The
Canadian Prairie
Cookbook

Jennifer Ogle • James Darcy • Jean Paré

Pictured on front cover: Tomato and Feta-stuffed Sirloin, p. 128

The Canadian Prairie Cookbook

Copyright © Company's Coming Publishing Limited

All rights reserved worldwide. No part of this book may be reproduced, stored in a retrieval system or transmitted in any form by any means without written permission in advance from the publisher.

In the case of photocopying or other reprographic copying, a license may be purchased from the Canadian Copyright Licensing Agency (Access Copyright). Visit www.accesscopyright.ca or call toll free 1-800-893-5777. In the United States, please contact the Copyright Clearance Centre at www.copyright.com or call 978-646-8600.

Brief portions of this book may be reproduced for review purposes, provided credit is given to the source. Reviewers are invited to contact the publisher for additional information.

First Printing June 2012

Library and Archives Canada Cataloguing in Publication

Ogle, Jennifer, 1972-

The Canadian prairie cookbook / Jennifer Ogle, James Darcy, Jean Paré.

(Canada cooks)

Includes index.

At head of title: Company's coming.

ISBN 978-1-897477-83-0

1. Cooking, Canadian--Prairie style. 2. Cooking--Prairie

Provinces. 3. Cookbooks-- I. Darcy, James II. Paré, Jean, 1927-

III. Title. IV. Series: Canada cooks series

TX715.6.O4522 2012   641.59712   C2011-907084-7

Portions of this book were previously published by Lone Pine Publishing as *The Alberta Seasonal Cookbook*, 2007, and *The Canadian Harvest Cookbook*, 2008. Company's Coming recipes contributed by Jean Paré: Fattoush; Beef and Spinach Pita Burgers; Spaghetti Arcobaleno; Prairie Pecan Tart; Roasted Potato Salad; Lemongrass Pork; Praline Pecans, Beets and Blue Cheese on Baby Greens; Tiramisu; Manitoba Wild Rice Salad; Ginger Beef; Sesame Chili Vegetable Skewers; Rhubarb Ginger Chutney; Grilled Chicken and Squash; Cabbage Rolls; and Spiced Rum Pear Cake.

Published by

Company's Coming Publishing Limited

2311 – 96 Street

Edmonton, Alberta, Canada T6N 1G3

Tel: 780-450-6223   Fax: 780-450-1857

www.companyscoming.com

Company's Coming is a registered trademark owned by Company's Coming Publishing Limited

We acknowledge the financial support of the Government of Canada through the Canada Book Fund for our publishing activities.

Printed in China

CONTENTS

The Company's Coming Legacy

Jean Paré grew up with an understanding that family, friends and home cooking are the key ingredients for a good life. A busy mother of four, Jean developed a knack for creating quick and easy recipes using everyday ingredients. For 18 years, she operated a successful catering business from her home kitchen in the small prairie town of Vermilion, Alberta, Canada. During that time, she earned a reputation for great food, courteous service and reasonable prices. Steadily increasing demand for her recipes led to the founding of Company's Coming Publishing Limited in 1981.

The first Company's Coming cookbook, *150 Delicious Squares*, was an immediate bestseller. As more titles were introduced, the company quickly earned the distinction of publishing Canada's most popular cookbooks. Company's Coming continues to gain new supporters in Canada, the United States and throughout the world by adhering to Jean's Golden Rule of Cooking: Never share a recipe you wouldn't use yourself. It's an approach that has worked—millions of times over!

A familiar and trusted name in the kitchen, Company's Coming has extended its reach throughout the home with other types of books and products for everyday living.

Though humble about her achievements, Jean Paré is one of North America's most loved and recognized authors. The recipient of many awards, Jean was appointed Member of the Order of Canada, her country's highest lifetime achievement honour.

Today, Jean Paré's influence as founding author, mentor and moral compass is evident in all aspects of the company she founded. Every recipe created and every product produced upholds the family values and work ethic she instilled. Readers the world over will continue to be encouraged and inspired by her legacy for generations to come.

INTRODUCTION

The Prairies are rich in locally grown, seasonally available products, including a diversity of meats, grains, fruit and vegetables. Artisanal cheese producers, microbreweries and specialty growers widen the variety even further. The Prairies are the proud home of Taber corn, Saskatchewan-grown lentils and Manitoba wild rice. Morels, chanterelles and other delicious mushrooms are available with a bit of knowledge and foraging. Trout and perch are among the fish native to our lakes.

Eating seasonally may seem an obvious idea, but how much do we really know about the food we eat every day? Where does it come from and how is it grown? What kind and how much fertilizer and pesticide remain on or in the product? Are the people who produce the food working with humane conditions and receiving adequate remuneration? Do we know the financial, ethical and environmental costs of transporting food around the world?

Prairie Pecan Tart, p. 36

Locally grown foods, often organically grown, are fresher and tastier and support our local economy. Farmers' markets across the Prairie provinces showcase our bounty, from simple foods such as tomatoes, strawberries, eggplant and garden peas to bison jerky and kimchi. Half the fun in spending part of a Saturday at your local market comes from being able to actually speak to the producers, who are more than

happy to explain how things are grown, give tips and even share family-tested recipes. Organic agriculture has grown some 20 percent a year over the past several years. Another source of locally grown products is your own backyard! Even if you have only a small plot of land or a balcony, you can grow many vegetables and fruits, and have plenty of fun doing it.

With this book, we have created a resource of recipes that represent the best of what the Prairies have to offer. It makes sense to buy Prairie beef, but try braising it when chestnuts are available in the fall. Seville oranges come into season in late January and February; those short, cold days are the best time to make some marmalade for a special treat. Saskatoons are available in late summer; use them to make a pie to end a Labour Day barbecue. It's all here, in the appetizers, salads, soups, main dishes, sides, desserts and snacks that make up the seasons of this book.

In Our Kitchen

We have found the following ingredient choices and cooking procedures to be successful in our kitchen and recommend them highly wherever possible.

Bay Leaves—Fresh leaves are occasionally available at large grocery stores and can be specially ordered. In a well-sealed container in the fridge, they can last three or four months.

Butter—Use unsalted; easiest to measure using the convenient markings on the wrapping.

Citrus Juices—Best fresh squeezed.

Coconut Milk—Use unsweetened coconut milk in cans. Naturally sweet, it is often better than cream in savoury dishes.

Eggs—Use large, free-run eggs. They should be at room temperature for baking.

Flour—Use unbleached all-purpose.

Various salts, clockwise from top left: Hawaiian salt, salt and peppercorns, pink salt, pure ocean salt, fleur de sel and kosher salt

Garlic—Use fresh garlic! If you can't be bothered to peel and chop fresh garlic you shouldn't be allowed to use it!

Herbs—Use fresh, unless stated otherwise. In a pinch, the best alternative to fresh is frozen, not dried. Freeze herbs yourself in the summer when they are plentiful, and you can even find them in the freezer section of some better grocery stores.

Lemons and Limes—Use fresh! You can't compare the taste to concentrate.

Mayonnaise—It's always better homemade:

5 egg yolks

⅔ cup (150 mL) extra virgin olive oil

¼ cup (60 mL) good quality vinegar or juice of 1 lemon

pinch of sea salt to taste

- You need both hands free to make mayonnaise. Spread a damp cloth on your counter, nestle a medium-sized bowl in its centre and wrap it around the base of the bowl to keep it steady while you whisk.

- Whisk yolk, vinegar and salt in bowl until well combined and yolk lightens in colour.

- Add oil, a drop at a time, whisking continuously until mixture emulsifies and thickens.

- When about half of oil has been added, add remaining oil in a slow, steady stream, whisking all the while. Store, covered, in refrigerator for up to 5 days. Thin if desired by lightly whisking in some water.

- Add mustard or fresh herbs if you like. Adding minced garlic turns plain mayonnaise into aioli. Makes just over 1 cup (250 mL).

Mushrooms—Morels and chanterelles can be found in the wild, but we advise that you confirm the identification of mushrooms with an experienced collector before cooking them; some species of mushrooms are acutely toxic and can cause death.

Mustard—Use good quality mustard for everything from sandwiches to dressings to sauces. When the last few teaspoons of mustard cling to the bottom of the jar, add fresh lemon juice, olive oil, sea salt and fresh pepper. Shake and use for salad dressing.

Oil, Sesame—Use for a nutty flavour addition. Store it in the fridge.

Oil, Olive—Extra virgin olive oil is indispensable. Try olive oil from Italy, Spain or Greece.

Oil, Grape Seed—Use for higher heat cooking.

Pepper, Fresh—Don't use pre-ground pepper; it has such poor flavour. A variety of peppercorns are available. Black or white can be used interchangeably in any of the recipes.

Brandied Seville Marmalade with Lemon and Ginger, p. 146

Roasted Potato Salad, p. 48

Salt—Brings out the flavour in food. Sea salt, kosher salt, Celtic salt—choose a favourite. Better yet, obtain some of each. Using a better-quality salt also means that you will use less, because the flavour is more intense. If you need to reduce salt even further for health reasons, use fresh herbs, various spices and flavour lifters, such as lemon juice, to maintain the flavour intensity while reducing the salt content.

Soy Sauce—Both tamari and shoyu are high quality, fermented and chemical-free "soy sauces" that are used to enhance flavour and impart a unique saltiness.

Star Anise—This strongly anise-scented Oriental spice is sold dried, as quarter-sized, star-shaped clusters of 5 to 10 pods, each containing a single seed. The seeds can be used on their own, crushed or ground, or the entire stars can be added, then removed before serving.

Stocks—Make homemade. Good quality stocks available in tetra packs are the best substitute. Miso, a fermented soybean paste, is another interesting alternative to stock, and it will keep in the refrigerator for several months. Stir it in 1 Tbsp (15 mL) at a time until you have a rich, full flavour.

Sugar—Use organic and unrefined rather than white and bleached. When looking for a rich brown sugar, use muscovado sugar, available in grocery and health food stores. It still contains the minerals and vitamins originally in the sugar cane plant, and it has a full molasses flavour.

Vinegar, Apple Cider—Use when you need an all-purpose vinegar; organic, unrefined and unpasteurized has the best flavour.

Vinegar, Balsamic—Great flavour in everything from soups to sweets. Be sure to try B.C.'s own balsamic such as Venturi Schulze of Okanagan Vinegar Brewery.

Yeast—Use regular dry yeast; ½ oz (15 g) dry yeast is equal to 1 Tbsp (15 mL) fresh yeast.

Measuring

Spoon dry ingredients into the measuring cup and level off with a knife or spatula.

Measurements are in both metric and imperial. Note that for butter, a pound is considered to be 454 g; for meat, vegetables, etc., a pound is 500 g.

Solids, including butter and most cheeses, are measured in dry-measure cups and liquids in liquid-measure cups.

Spring Heirloom Tomato Salad

Serves 4

If you are interested in tomatoes that remind you of days in the garden as a child picking the sun-warmed fruit right off the vine, look no further than Hotchkiss tomatoes. Grown on a Calgary area family-owned farm dedicated to growing heirloom tomatoes, over 30 varieties of Hotchkiss can be found at high-end restaurants and specialty markets across the province. Growers throughout the Prairies produce fine heirloom varieties of tomatoes. Tomatoes (*Solanum lycopersicum*) are native to the Americas and were brought to Europe in the 16th century. Although the Europeans admired tomatoes for their beauty, they initially believed the entire plant to be poisonous. The leaves and stems do indeed contain toxic compounds, but the fruits are quite edible. Other sources say the reason for the tomato's slow acceptance at European dinner tables was because the lead in pewter plates reacted with the fruit, causing it to leach into the tomatoes.

1 clove garlic, minced

splash of white balsamic vinegar

¼ cup (60 mL) olive oil

sea salt and freshly ground pepper to taste

1 lb (500 g) heirloom tomatoes, washed, cored and sliced ½ in (1.25 cm) thick

½ lb (250 g) bocconcini, sliced ½ in (1.25 cm) thick

handful of fresh basil leaves, washed and patted dry

crusty French baguette

In a salad bowl, add garlic, vinegar and olive oil. Then add tomatoes, tossing gently to coat with dressing. Season to taste with salt and pepper.

On individual plates, layer tomato slices with bocconcini and some basil tucked in between and around tomato slices. Scatter remaining basil leaves on top and drizzle with remaining dressing.

Serve with slices of baguette.

Tip

Fresh tomatoes from the garden or the farmers' market would also work in this recipe.

Bocconcini is a semi-ripe mozzarella cheese that comes in small, soft, white balls.

In her tomato book, the late Lois Hole, beloved lieutenant-governor of Alberta and long-time gardening guru, wrote about the importance of heirloom varieties in maintaining gene pool diversity. Lois called this contribution priceless because the heirloom seeds are used in developing new varieties that have natural resistance to viral, fungal and bacterial diseases.

Asparagus and Chèvre Salad

Serves 4

The Prairie provinces are dotted with artisan cheese producers. For example, Bothwell Cheese, located south of Winnipeg, started making quality cheese in 1936. Natricia Dairy, in the heart of Alberta's dairy land, is one of the region's largest producers of goat cheese. *Chèvre* is the French word for "goat," and it has become synonymous with the French-style, tangy, fluffy, soft cheese made from goat's milk. Most grocery-store varieties are mild, moist and creamy and come in logs or cylinders, sometimes rolled in herbs or spices such as peppercorns, or coated with ash or edible leaves. Goat's milk can also be made into other types of cheese, including feta, Gouda and Brie. As well, chèvre can be fashioned into other shapes, such as pyramids. Somewhat more piquant in taste than cheeses made with cow's milk, chèvre is often more easily digested by people with lactose intolerance; it also has twice the protein and one-third the calories.

1 bunch (about 2 lb [1 kg]) asparagus, trimmed

splash of olive oil

sea salt and freshly ground pepper to taste

1 lb (500 g) package frozen peas, refreshed in boiling water, drained and cooled

1 cup (250 g) chèvre, crumbled

½ cup (125 mL) chopped fresh mint

½ cup (125 mL) chopped fresh basil

1 lime, cut into 4 wedges

Preheat barbecue to medium-high heat. Toss asparagus with olive oil, salt and pepper. Grill for 4 minutes, turning once. Set aside.

In a bowl, toss together remaining ingredients, except lime. Cut the warm asparagus into bite-sized pieces and add to bowl. Toss and season again if needed. (You cut the asparagus after because it is much easier to grill if left whole!) Divide among 4 plates and garnish each salad with a lime wedge.

Tip

Soft cheeses such as chèvre do not slice well, often ending up as a crumbled mess that sticks to the knife. The easiest way to cut a soft cheese is with a piece of taut dental floss—just be sure to use unflavoured!

Tip

Allow cheese to come to room temperature for at least 30 minutes (longer for hard cheese or if the room is particularly cold) before serving in order to enjoy its full flavour and aroma. Portion cheese, if desired, while cold and keep it wrapped so it doesn't dry out before you are ready to serve.

Fattoush

Serves 4

Spring radishes, such as the familiar round, red radish, are often used in salads. You can either pick them up at farmers' markets or grow them yourself: many varieties are ready in less than a month. This Asian-inspired salad from the Company's Coming collection is perfect for spring! Bright, tangy flavours and crisp textures combine for a fresh taste.

1 whole-wheat pita bread (7 in [18 cm] diameter)

1 tsp (5 mL) + 1/3 cup (75 mL) extra virgin olive oil

2 tsp (10 mL) za'atar spice blend (see Tip)

4 cups (1 L) shredded romaine lettuce, lightly packed

1 cup (250 mL) diced Lebanese cucumber

1 cup (250 mL) diced seeded Roma (plum) tomato

1/2 cup (125 mL) sliced radish

1/3 cup (75 mL) chopped fresh mint

1/3 cup (75 mL) chopped fresh parsley

1/3 cup (75 mL) diced green pepper

1/3 cup (75 mL) thinly sliced red onion (1 in [2.5 cm] pieces)

1/3 cup (75 mL) lemon juice

1/2 tsp (2 mL) grated lemon zest

1 clove garlic, minced

1 tsp (5 mL) salt

1/4 tsp (1 mL) pepper

Brush both sides of pita with 1 tsp (5 mL) olive oil and sprinkle with za'atar. Bake directly on centre rack in a 325° F (160° C) oven for 10 minutes per side until crisp and dry. Cool on a wire rack. Break into 1 in (2.5 cm) pieces and put into a bowl.

Add romaine lettuce, cucumber, tomato, radish, mint, parsley, green pepper and red onion.

Combine 1/3 cup (75 mL) olive oil, lemon juice, lemon zest, garlic, salt and pepper. Drizzle over salad and toss.

Tip

Use a very sharp knife or scissors to chop mint and parsley so the leaves are cleanly cut, not bruised. Mint is especially susceptible to blackened edges if not cut cleanly.

Tip

Put the vegetables and herbs into the bottom of the bowl with the lettuce lightly set on top, cover with plastic wrap and refrigerate for up to four hours. Toss with the dressing and pita. Prepare and refrigerate dressing up to two days in advance, but bring to room temperature before combining with the salad ingredients because the olive oil will solidify a bit in the fridge.

Tip

Za'atar spice blend, also spelled *satar* or *zahatar,* is a herb blend used extensively throughout the Middle East. Za'atar is commonly made of marjoram, oregano, thyme, toasted seeds and salt.

Lebanese cucumbers are like miniature English cucumbers. They're small (usually no longer than 5 to 6 in [12 to 15 cm]), almost seedless, sweet and juicy and are eaten with the deep green peel left on. Unpeeled English cucumbers can be used in their place.

Lobster Cocktail

Serves 6

"Surf 'n' turf," also known as steak and lobster, became a popular menu item in steakhouses across the Prairies in the boom years of the 1970s. Surf 'n' turf has evolved to include any combo of seafood and meat, but the pairing of our favourite red meat and the succulent lobster remains a fixture on menus throughout the Prairies. Spring marks the start of lobster season in Atlantic Canada, and spring lobsters are regarded as the best quality because of their thick shells, high meat content and excellent taste.

1 x 8 oz (250 g) lobster, fresh or frozen (thawed and squeezed of excess liquid)

3 Tbsp (45 mL) mayonnaise

1 tsp (5 mL) mustard

1 Tbsp (15 mL) fresh mint, chopped

1 Tbsp (15 mL) fresh tarragon, chopped

½ tsp (2 mL) lime zest

½ tsp (2 mL) orange zest

juice of ½ lime

1 tsp (5 mL) horseradish, or more to taste

1 Tbsp (15 mL) capers, squeezed dry and chopped

⅓ cup (75 mL) roasted red bell pepper, diced small

sea salt and freshly ground pepper to taste

Avocado Mix

1 avocado, peeled and cubed into small dice

juice of ½ lime

Garnish

sliced green onions or caviar

Mix lobster, mayonnaise and remaining ingredients, and season with salt and pepper.

For avocado mix, toss avocado cubes in lime juice in a separate bowl. To serve, layer lobster with avocado. Garnish with green onions or caviar and serve as an appetizer with your favourite crackers. Makes approximately 3 cups (750 mL).

Spicy horseradish (Armoracia rusticana) *is the root of a perennial herb native to Europe and Asia—the aroma alone is enough to make a grown man cry.*

Now naturalized in North America, horseradish can be very difficult to eradicate once planted in your garden. It grows wild in Alberta, and starting in late spring, is available at local farmers' markets. It adds zip to this lobster cocktail.

Cipollini and Asiago-stuffed Morels

Serves 4 as an appetizer

Alberta is the proud home of the only mycological club in Canada's prairie provinces, the Edmonton Mycological Society. The organization holds an annual morel forage in May, with forays throughout the year in the Rocky Mountain foothills, northern Aspen Parkland and southern Boreal Forest ecozones of Alberta. Highly prized for their meaty, mushroomy flavour, morels (*Morchella*) are edible cup fungi. Morels generally grow year after year on the same forested sites, preferring the company of ash trees, but they flourish in the years immediately following a forest fire. Another mushroom worth mentioning is Alberta's official mushroom (as of 2009), the red cap mushroom (*Leccinum boreale*).

1 Tbsp (15 mL) grape seed oil or canola oil

½ cup (125 mL) cipollini onion, peeled and quartered

1 lb (500 g) fresh morels, reserve 12 of the largest ones left whole, the rest chopped for stuffing

¼ cup (60 mL) white wine

1 clove garlic, minced

¼ cup (60 mL) parsley, chopped

2 Tbsp (30 mL) chives, chopped

¼ cup (60 mL) grated Asiago cheese

2 to 3 Tbsp (30 to 45 mL) panko

sea salt and pepper to taste

(continued on next page)

In a medium saucepan, heat grape seed oil over medium heat and sauté cipollini onion until it starts to caramelize, about 5 minutes. Add chopped mushrooms and white wine and cook for about 5 minutes. Add garlic and cook for 2 to 3 minutes. Remove pan from heat. Stir in remaining ingredients, except for the 12 reserved morels. Stuff reserved morels with the filling.

For lime mayonnaise, stir together lime zest and mayonnaise. Set aside.

For breading, place flour, eggs and panko into separate bowls. Heat clarified butter in a saucepan over medium-high heat. Bread stuffed morels one at a time, dipping first in flour, then egg and finally panko. Cook mushrooms in butter until brown and crispy. Serve hot with lime mayonnaise.

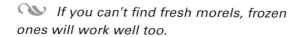 *If you can't find fresh morels, frozen ones will work well too.*

Tip

To remove any unwanted critters hiding in the morels, soak mushrooms in salted water for at least one hour.

Tip

To make clarified butter, melt unsalted butter slowly over low heat. Gradually, froth will rise to the top with a layer of clear golden oil in the middle and a layer of milk solids on the bottom. Clarified butter is the middle layer. Skim off the froth and carefully ladle out the clear oil, leaving out the milk solids.

Lime Mayonnaise

zest from 1 lime

½ cup (125 mL) mayonnaise

Breading

½ cup (125 mL) flour

3 eggs, lightly beaten

2 cups (500 mL) panko

1 cup (250 mL) clarified butter (see Tip)

Panko is a coarser variety of bread crumb, and has a crispier texture when fried. It can be found in Asian markets.

Cream of Asparagus Soup

Serves 6

With a short season extending from May to the end of June, fresh asparagus (*Asparagus officinalis*) offers a much-anticipated break from the winter blues. Asparagus is a member of the lily family. The name most likely comes from either the Persian word *asparag*, meaning sprout, or from the Greek word *aspharagos*, meaning "long as one's throat." It grows well in our cooler climate, and it is even said that plants can survive for decades on the Prairies in a cultivated field or as a roadside weed. Edgar Farm, located in Innisfail, Alberta, has the largest field of asparagus in the province, a full 17 acres (7 hectares) of it. The Edgars have discovered that by sacrificing some yield and using the cool weather to their advantage, they can produce a delicious, sweeter-than-normal asparagus. Check out farmers' markets and U-pick gardens for fresh asparagus starting in May.

2 Tbsp (30 mL) unsalted butter

2 Tbsp (30 mL) olive oil

1 large yellow onion, diced

¼ cup (60 mL) white wine

2 sweet potatoes, diced

½ tsp (2 mL) fresh thyme, chopped

¼ cup (60 mL) parsley, chopped

2 stalks celery, diced

2 cloves garlic, minced

sea salt to taste

8 cups (2 L) chicken or vegetable stock

1 cup (250 mL) heavy cream (32%)

2 lbs (1 kg) fresh asparagus, roughly chopped, reserve some tips for garnish

1 cup (250 mL) packed fresh spinach

fresh lemon juice

In a medium pot, heat butter and oil. Add onion and sauté until golden. Add white wine and bring to a rapid boil on high heat until liquid is reduced, about 3 to 5 minutes. Add sweet potatoes, thyme, parsley, celery, garlic, salt and stock and bring to a boil. Immediately reduce heat to a simmer and cook until sweet potatoes are soft, about 15 minutes.

Add cream, asparagus and spinach, and bring to a gentle simmer. When the asparagus are tender, about 5 minutes, remove from heat and purée in a blender until smooth. Season with a good squeeze of fresh lemon juice. Taste and adjust seasoning. Serve hot in bowls with a garnish of heavy cream seasoned with a pinch of salt and a splash of fresh lemon juice on top.

(continued on next page)

Tip

By snapping off the lower ends of the asparagus, you ensure that you are getting the most tender part of the spear. Alternatively, you can use a vegetable peeler: start about two-thirds from the bottom end and peel the more fibrous outer layer, exposing the tender flesh.

Tip

Store asparagus upright in about 1 in (2.5 cm) of water. Keep asparagus refrigerated because the sugars can turn to starch quickly.

Variation

White asparagus tastes the same as green asparagus and can be used in the same ways. Rarer and thus more expensive, white asparagus is grown by keeping the tender shoots covered with soil and away from sunlight.

Garnish

¼ cup (60 mL) heavy cream (32%)

pinch of sea salt

fresh lemon juice

Broccoli and Tempeh Rice Bowl

Serves 4

In the Prairies, fresh local broccoli becomes available in June and, weather permitting, can last through the first two weeks of October. A member of the cabbage family, broccoli (*Brassica oleracea*) is a very close relative of cauliflower. Not that long ago in the Prairies, broccoli was an unfamiliar vegetable favoured by our Italian immigrants. (In fact, it was eaten in what is now Tuscany long before it was eaten anywhere else, and it was adopted by the Romans when they invaded the region.) When it first came to Great Britain, broccoli was known as "Italian asparagus." Nowadays, broccoli makes the grade as a popular superfood—it is loaded with vitamins and the anti-cancer enzyme sulforaphane. "Canadian broccoli," otherwise known as "Russian Red," although a member of the same family of vegetables, is not broccoli at all, but a type of kale.

2 Tbsp (30 mL) soy sauce

1 Tbsp (30 mL) mirin or sweet rice wine

2 Tbsp (30 mL) light miso

1 tsp (5 mL) toasted sesame oil

¼ tsp (1 mL) cornstarch

2 tsp (10 mL) grape seed oil or canola oil

1 Tbsp (15 mL) ginger, finely chopped

2 tsp (10 mL) lemongrass, tender bottom part only, chopped

2 cloves garlic, minced

1 package Indonesian-style tempeh, cut into ½ in (1.25 cm) strips

(continued on next page)

In a small bowl, combine soy sauce, mirin, miso, sesame oil and cornstarch, stirring with a whisk. Set aside.

Heat grape seed oil or canola oil in a large skillet over medium-high heat and sauté ginger, lemongrass and garlic for 1 minute or just until mixture begins to brown. Add tempeh and sauté for 2 minutes.

Add broccoli, peppers, snow peas and sauté for 1 minute. Add to skillet and cook for 1 minute until sauce has slightly thickened. Remove from heat and stir in green onions, sesame seeds and salt. Serve over rice.

Tip

Soak your broccoli in warm, salted water to get rid of any critters. As with all members of the cabbage family, broccoli is best used within a few days of picking to retain its sweet flavour and mild odour.

Tempeh is a fermented soybean product that has been enjoyed in Southeast Asia for centuries. It is fermented with a Rhizopus mould, which makes the soy protein more easily digestible. Tempeh has a deep, nutty flavour and can be used in meals as a substitute for tofu or meat. Here in the Prairies, it is available at most supermarkets.

1 head of broccoli, cut into florets

½ cup (125 mL) each yellow and red pepper, cut into strips

½ cup (125 mL) snow peas

½ cup (125 mL) green onions, cut in ¼ in (6 mm) diagonal strips

2 tsp (10 mL) black sesame seeds

½ tsp (2 mL) sea salt

2 cups (500 mL) hot, cooked brown rice

Beef and Spinach Pita Burgers

Serves 4

Spinach is a great vegetable to grow on the Prairies—it requires little effort and is ready early in the season. It likes cool weather and can even tolerate a light frost, which is very handy when our spring temperatures unexpectedly take a quick dive overnight. Best yet, spinach is considered a "superfood"—it's packed full of nutrients and vitamins and has been linked to more health benefits than perhaps any other food in the world. It's a great source of calcium and helps build strong bones, and has also demonstrated anticancer properties. This simple recipe from the Company's Coming collection features spinach alongside our world-famous Prairie beef.

¼ cup (60 mL) crumbled feta cheese

¼ cup (60 mL) fine dry bread crumbs

¼ cup (60 mL) finely chopped black olives

1 tsp (5 mL) dried oregano

1 tsp (5 mL) grated lemon zest

1 clove garlic, minced

½ tsp (2 mL) salt

1 lb (500 g) lean ground beef

½ cup (125 mL) roasted red pepper hummus

4 pita breads (7 in [18 cm] diameter), warmed (see Tip)

1 cup (250 mL) spinach leaves (stems removed), lightly packed

Combine feta, bread crumbs, olives, oregano, lemon zest, garlic, salt and ground beef and divide into 4 portions. Shape portions into half moon–shaped patties. Grill on barbecue on direct medium heat for about 9 minutes per side until internal temperature reaches 160° F (71° C).

Spread hummus over pitas, arranging spinach over half of each pita. Place patties over spinach and fold pitas in half to enclose.

Tip

To warm the pita breads, wrap in foil and place on upper rack of barbecue or directly on the grill. Remove when just headed through.

Serve this Greek-inspired barbecue dish with a medley of fresh seasonal vegetables that are tossed with a bit of olive oil.

Prairie Lamb with Mustard Spaetzle

Serves 4

Sheep farming had a tumultuous start here on the Prairies, which may explain why lamb is not as popular today as beef and chicken. By 1884 the battle between cattle ranchers and sheep farmers had grown bitter and the federal government, in support of the cattlemen, banned sheep in southwestern Alberta from the U.S. border north to the Bow River. However, many of today's large cattle farms in southern Saskatchewan got their start as sheep ranches. Today, lamb is becoming more and more popular, with Prairie lamb making it onto the menus of the great restaurants in the country. The organization Canadian Prairie Lamb, based out of Saskatchewan, produces a number of value-added lamb products, such as appetizers. When purchasing Prairie lamb, look for lamb that has been grain-fed, not grass-fed: this gives the lamb a uniquely mild flavour compared to lamb grown elsewhere in the world. It is believed that sheep were domesticated by 8900 BC, in the area that is now Iraq and Romania. Of course, some of the oldest recipes for lamb come from Greece, where lamb is still a favourite.

2 x 1½ lb (680 g) lamb racks, frenched (trimmed and ready to use; available in most grocery stores)

2 Tbsp (30 mL) extra virgin olive oil

sea salt and freshly ground pepper

1 clove garlic, minced

1 cup (250 mL) chopped fresh parsley

2 Tbsp (30 mL) *each* chopped fresh thyme and rosemary

¼ cup (60 mL) bread crumbs

¼ cup (60 mL) Dijon mustard

(continued on next page)

Place a heavy-bottomed pan over medium-high heat. Brush lamb with oil and season with salt and pepper. Sear lamb until brown on all sides. Remove from heat and let sit 15 minutes.

Preheat oven to 450° F (230° C). Mix garlic and herbs together in a bowl with bread crumbs. Place lamb on a small rimmed baking sheet; brush Dijon mustard on rounded side of lamb. Divide breadcrumb mixture evenly over mustard to form a crust. Bake for 10 to 15 minutes or until a thermometer inserted in centre reaches 140° F (60° C) for medium-rare. Let rest 5 to 10 minutes before cutting into chops.

For the spaetzle, bring a large pot of salted water to a boil. Set a bowl of ice water near pot. Sift flour and salt together. Whisk together eggs, milk and Dijon mustard and pour into flour, stirring to make a smooth batter. Using a spaetzle maker or food mill, drop batter into boiling water. When spaetzle comes to surface, transfer to ice water with a slotted spoon. Repeat until all batter is used. As they cool, remove spaetzle from water and place in sieve to drain. To reheat spaetzle, toss them in hot butter or sauce—or fry them over medium heat until golden.

Spaetzle or spätzle ("little sparrow") are dumplings very similar to pasta. They are served as a side dish and are common fare, especially in southern Germany and the Alsace region. Spaetzle makers are available at specialty food shops, department stores and German markets (where you will likely find a good one for a reasonable price).

Spaetzle

1¼ cups (310 mL) flour

1 tsp (5 mL) sea salt

3 large eggs

⅓ cup (75 mL) milk

1 Tbsp (15 mL) grainy Dijon mustard

Spaghetti Arcobaleno

Serves 6 to 8

This light pasta dish from Jean Paré's collection features an *arcobaleno* (Italian for "rainbow") of fresh spring ingredients, including fresh basil. Basil *(Ocimum basilicum)* thrives in the heat of summer, and it will grow in abundance if it is kept in a humid environment. It does not tolerate cold weather, so when growing basil on the Prairies, be sure there is no chance of frost. It can also be planted indoors, preferably in a south-facing window. Basil is thought to have originated in India, where it was considered a holy plant and often planted near shrines and temples. Legend has it that the Greeks named the plant βασιλεύς, meaning "king," when it was found growing above the spot where the Holy Cross was rediscovered in the 4th century AD. Even today, basil is considered the high priest of herbs. There are dozens of varieties available, from licorice basil and cinnamon-flavoured basil to purple varieties and spicy warm ones, such as Thai basil.

8 oz (225 g) spaghetti

Cook pasta according to package directions. Drain.

1 tsp (5 mL) olive oil

1 lb (500 g) salmon fillets, skin and any small bones removed

Heat olive oil in a large frying pan on medium. Add salmon. Cook for about 4 minutes per side until fish flakes easily when tested with a fork. Transfer to a plate. Cover to keep warm.

2 cups (500 mL) halved grape tomatoes

1½ cups (375 mL) chopped yellow pepper

1 cup (250 mL) whole pitted kalamata olives

½ cup (125 mL) dry (or alcohol-free) white wine

½ cup (125 mL) sun-dried tomato pesto

¼ tsp (1 mL) salt

Add grape tomatoes, yellow pepper, olives, wine, pesto and salt to same frying pan. Bring to a boil. Cook for about 10 minutes, stirring occasionally, until yellow pepper is tender.

Add asparagus and pasta. Stir. Cook, covered, for about 1 minute until asparagus is tender-crisp. Transfer to a large serving bowl. Break up salmon pieces. Add to pasta mixture. Add basil, lemon juice, lemon zest and pepper. Toss.

(continued on next page)

Tip

When a recipe calls for grated zest and juice, it's easier to grate the fruit first, then juice it. Be careful not to grate down to the pith (white part of the peel), which is bitter and best avoided.

2 cups (500 mL) chopped fresh asparagus (1 in [2.5 cm] pieces)

½ cup (125 mL) chopped fresh basil or 2 Tbsp (30 mL) dried basil

1 Tbsp (30 mL) lemon juice

1 tsp (5 mL) grated lemon zest (see Tip)

¼ tsp (1 mL) pepper

Potato Frittata

Serves 4

Potatoes have always formed part of the backbone of the Prairie diet. Cheap, easy to cook and tasty, they are a comfort food and adapt well in many recipes. Canada has around 360,000 acres (145,700 hectares) of land dedicated to potato growing. Manitoba is the second-largest grower in the country, after Prince Edward Island. Alberta comes in fourth, and Saskatchewan has a small commercial potato industry as well. The average Canadian eats about 163 pounds (74 kilograms) of potatoes per year—which is about the same as all the other vegetables the average Canadian eats put together! From the Italian word *fritto* ("fried"), a frittata is an open-faced omelette made with cheese and other ingredients mixed into the eggs. It is a classic Roman dish traditionally served on Easter Day. Incorporating potatoes into this breakfast dish makes it an especially satisfying and comforting one-dish meal.

2 Tbsp (30 mL) butter

3 onions, sliced

2 medium Yukon Gold potatoes, peeled, cooked and sliced

8 eggs

¾ cup (175 mL) cream or milk

sea salt and freshly ground black pepper

½ cup (125 mL) aged Cheddar cheese, grated

1 Tbsp (15 mL) fresh thyme, chopped

Preheat broiler to 500° F (260° C). Melt butter in a 9 in (23 cm) nonstick, ovenproof pan over low heat. Add onions and sauté, stirring occasionally, for 10 to 15 minutes until onions are golden brown. Add potato slices and cook until starting to brown, about 5 minutes. Whisk eggs, cream or milk, salt and pepper in a bowl to combine. Pour egg mixture over onions in frying pan and sprinkle with cheese and thyme. Cook frittata for 5 to 6 minutes or until it is almost set. To finish cooking, place frittata under broiler for 1 minute. Cut into wedges and serve along with your breakfast favourites.

The Yukon Gold potato, now the favourite of chefs around the world for its texture, flavour and tempting golden flesh, was bred by Canadian Gary Johnston and his colleagues at the University of Guelph in the 1960s.

Braised Swiss Chard

Serves 4 as a side dish

This cool-climate vegetable is an ideal Prairie vegetable, as it can withstand frost, and when planted in early spring, it is usually ready to eat within four to six weeks. It also rivals spinach as a great leafy green because, unlike spinach, it contains no oxalic acid, allowing the minerals it contains to be more readily digestible. Chard (*Beta vulgaris* var. *cicla;* sometimes known as silverbeet) is a kind of beet grown for its leaves rather than its roots. Chard is naturally high in sodium—1 cup (250 mL) contains 313 mg—but it also packs a huge amount of vitamin A. It is indigenous to the Mediterranean, but it is called Swiss chard as a result of its initial scientific description in the 16th century by a Swiss botanist.

2 small red onions, chopped

1 Tbsp (15 mL) butter

2 lbs (1 kg) chard leaves, stems removed

¼ cup (60 mL) white wine

sea salt and freshly ground pepper to taste

Sauté onions in butter over medium heat in a large pan until they are nearly softened and lightly browned, about 8 to 10 minutes.

Meanwhile, clean chard leaves (see Tip) and slice into ribbons. Add chard leaves and wine. Cook rapidly, stirring frequently, until chard is wilted and liquid has evaporated, about 5 minutes.

Season with salt and pepper.

Tip

To clean chard, simply swish in cool water and pat dry. The stems and leaves are both edible, but should be cooked separately because the stems take longer to cook.

Chard can be used instead of spinach or kale in your favourite recipes.

The tasty braised swiss chard is pictured here with simple beef skewers. Swiss chard makes for a great—and somewhat unusual—accompaniment for a number of main dishes.

Asparagus Omelette

Serves 1

Eggs have long been associated with spring, rebirth and immortality. In many cultures, Easter eggs are elaborately decorated and given as gifts, the most extravagant being the Fabergé eggs of the Russian tsars. Perhaps the most famous decorated eggs are the pysanka. These eggs, decorated using the written-wax batik method that dates back to the Trypillian culture, continue to be hugely popular in many central and eastern European countries. In Ukraine, it is believed that the fate of the world rests on the continuation of the pysanka tradition. In Vegreville, this belief has been taken very seriously: in 1974 the town erected the world's largest pysanka, which is surely one of the most popular of the many *big* Prairie roadside attractions. As far as edible eggs are concerned, the Prairie provinces have active egg production industries, with a growing percentage being organic and free-range. According to the Manitoba Egg Farmers, there are nearly 170 registered egg farmers in Manitoba alone.

3 eggs, separated

2 Tbsp (30 mL) cream (10 to 18%)

1 Tbsp (15 mL) unsalted butter

pinch sea salt and freshly ground pepper

6 thin (or 3 thick) asparagus stalks, lightly steamed

2 Tbsp (30 mL) Boursin cheese (Garlic and Fine Herbs or Pepper)

1 Tbsp (15 mL) fresh chopped chives

In a medium bowl, blend egg yolks and cream with a fork. In another bowl, beat whites until soft peaks form. Gently fold whites into yolks. In a nonstick 10 in (25 cm) pan, melt butter over medium-high heat. Pour in eggs, swirling around pan to distribute evenly. Season with salt and pepper. Using a spatula, push eggs gently around to allow uncooked egg to flow underneath. Run spatula around sides of omelette to loosen. When omelette is almost set, about 40 seconds, lay asparagus and cheese in middle of omelette. Fold one-third of omelette over filling, then lift pan and slide opposite third onto your plate. Fold omelette onto itself, forming a neat tri-fold package. Sprinkle with chives and serve immediately.

Tip

When buying asparagus, choose firm, bright green stalks for the best flavour.

Asparagus is an excellent source of folic acid, vitamin C and antioxidants.

Hot Cross Buns

Makes 12

For many Prairie residents, Easter wouldn't be the same without spicy, sweet hot cross buns. Eaten in many Christian countries on Good Friday, hot cross buns are adorned with a cross (often made of pastry or icing) that symbolizes the crucifixion of Christ. The origins of the bun are likely a mixture of Christian and pagan traditions. One story is that during the Lenten season, Queen Elizabeth I of England attempted to ban the buns along with Roman Catholicism. When it became evident that the practice of putting a cross on buns could not be stopped, she passed a law that limited consumption of the buns to certain religious ceremonies. Supporters of hot cross buns at the time claimed that the buns would not rise without the cross, leading some culinary historians to believe that the first hot cross buns were scored with a knife, rather than decorated with pastry. Whatever their origin, hot cross buns are a welcome treat after the long Lenten fast.

1 Tbsp (15 mL) quick-rise yeast

¼ cup (60 mL) sugar

¼ cup (60 mL) warm water

2 cups (500 mL) unbleached bread flour

⅓ cup (75 mL) stone-ground whole-grain bread flour

1 tsp (5 mL) sea salt

½ tsp (2 mL) *each* dried cinnamon, coriander and lavender

½ tsp (2 mL) freshly grated nutmeg

2 Tbsp (30 mL) cold unsalted butter, diced

⅓ cup (75 mL) currants

¼ cup (60 mL) golden raisins

¼ cup (60 mL) mixed fruit peel, finely chopped

1 large egg, beaten

1 cup (250 mL) milk

Prepare 1 parchment paper–lined baking sheet.

Put yeast and 1 Tbsp (15 mL) of sugar in a small bowl with warm water until dissolved. Let sit 10 minutes.

Combine flours, salt and spices in a bowl. Add diced butter and rub into flour using tips of your fingers until mixture looks like fine crumbs. Mix in currants, golden raisins and mixed fruit peel, then make a well in the centre of mixture.

Add yeast mixture, remaining sugar and beaten egg to well, and approximately half of milk. Gradually add enough milk to flour–fruit mixture to make a soft, but not sticky, dough. Add more milk, if necessary, or extra flour, if dough is too sticky.

Turn dough onto a lightly floured work surface and knead thoroughly for 10 minutes.

Return dough to bowl and then cover bowl with plastic wrap. Let rise in a warm spot in kitchen until doubled in size, about 1½ hours.

Punch down dough a couple of times to deflate and divide into 12 equal pieces. Shape each into a neat ball and set well apart on the baking sheet. Slip baking sheet into large plastic bags and let rise as before until doubled in size, 45 minutes to 1 hour.

(continued on next page)

Meanwhile, preheat oven to 400° F (200° C). To make dough for cross pattern, put flour, butter and sugar into a small bowl and rub butter into flour with your fingertips until mixture looks like coarse crumbs. Stir in cold water and mix; dough will be firm. Roll pastry into a long, thin rope about $\frac{1}{8}$ in (3 mm) thick and cut into segments approximately 3 in (7.5 cm) long.

When buns are ready, uncover and brush with a little water to dampen, then place cross pattern on top of buns. Bake for 15 to 20 minutes until golden brown.

Meanwhile, to prepare glaze, combine honey and milk until smooth. As soon as buns are done, place them on a cooling rack and brush immediately with hot glaze. Eat warm or toasted, or freeze for up to 1 month.

Pastry Cross

$\frac{1}{3}$ cup (75 mL) white flour

scant $\frac{1}{4}$ cup (60 mL) cold unsalted butter, diced

2 tsp (10 mL) sugar

1 to 2 Tbsp (15 to 30 mL) cold water

Glaze

3 Tbsp (45 mL) honey

3 Tbsp (45 mL) milk

Prairie Pecan Tart

Serves 8

The maple syrup and Canadian whisky in this classic tart from Company's Coming are quintessentially Canadian ingredients. Most of our maple syrup is from Quebec. First Nations peoples were the first to harvest the sap of maple trees. Each year, they set up sugar camps in the mid-altitude maple groves of northeastern North American and used buckets made from birch to collect the sap. Explorer Jacques Cartier, in the 16th century, was the first to describe the acquisition of maple sap. Many Canadian whiskies are produced with Canadian Prairie wheat and rye. The award-winning Alberta Premium, distilled in Calgary, is one of only a few 100% rye grain varieties.

1¼ cups (310 mL) all-purpose flour

⅓ cup (75 mL) cold butter (or hard margarine), cut up

¼ cup (60 mL) finely chopped pecans

2 Tbsp (30 mL) + 1 cup (250 mL) brown sugar, packed

¼ tsp (1 mL) salt

⅓ cup (75 mL) Canadian whisky (rye), *divided*

2 Tbsp (30 mL) ice water

1¼ cups (300 mL) pecan halves

3 large eggs, fork-beaten

½ cup (125 mL) maple syrup

3 Tbsp (45 mL) butter (or hard margarine), melted

Process flour, butter, pecans, 2 Tbsp (30 mL) brown sugar and salt in food processor until mixture resembles coarse crumbs.

Add 2 Tbsp (30 mL) whisky and water. Process with on/off motion until mixture starts to come together. Do not over process. Turn out onto lightly floured surface. Press pastry into ball. Flatten slightly into disc. Wrap with plastic wrap. Chill for 30 minutes. Remove plastic wrap. Roll out pastry on lightly floured surface to fit ungreased 9 in (23 cm) tart pan with fluted sides and removable bottom. Carefully lift pastry and press into bottom and up sides of tart pan. Trim edge. Poke pastry several times with a fork. Chill for 1 hour. Place pan on ungreased baking sheet with sides (see Tip). Bake on bottom rack in 375° F (190° C) oven for about 25 minutes until golden. Cool.

Scatter pecan halves in pie shell.

Whisk eggs, 1 cup (250 mL) brown sugar, maple syrup, butter and 3 Tbsp (45 mL) whisky in medium bowl until smooth. Pour over pecans. Bake on bottom rack in 350° F (175° C) oven for about 30 minutes until golden and set. Let stand in pan on wire rack until cool.

Tip

Placing the tart pan on a baking sheet provides a safe way to transfer the hot pan out of the oven.

Birch syrup can be tapped from mature white birch (Betula papyrifera). *The flavour is slightly more bittersweet and is lighter in colour than maple syrup. There are a few birch syrup producers across the Prairies.*

Ruth's Unbaked Strawberry Cheesecake

Serves 8

The name "strawberry" is derived from the Old English *streawberige*, with *streaw* meaning "straw" and *berige* meaning "berry." In parts of northern Europe, wild berries are still commonly gathered by threading them onto a straw, giving a possible origin for the name. Historically, the strawberries (*Fragaria* species) of Europe were probably not widely eaten—although they were used occasionally for medicine, and the plants did become popular with the French nobility for their flowers. By the 1400s, strawberries were being sold on the streets of London. The importation of a large Chilean species of strawberry to Europe in 1714 was the first step in developing the large strawberries we now know and love. Strawberries, which are ready for harvest by the beginning of July, are a good source of vitamin C. They grow well in our climate and are the first local fruit of the season. The Prairies are blessed with many U-pick farms that feature strawberries, and strawberries are also easy to grow in a container garden on your deck or balcony. This recipe is an unbaked cheesecake, which is creamier and not as heavy as baked cheesecakes, and it's more suited to juicy strawberries.

Crust

2 cups (500 mL) graham wafer crumbs

½ cup (125 mL) + 1 Tbsp (15 mL) unsalted butter, melted

zest of 1 lemon, finely chopped

Filling

3 x 250 g packages cream cheese, at room temperature

½ to 1 cup (125 to 250 mL) icing sugar, sifted

fresh lemon juice

⅓ cup (75 mL) whipping cream (32%)

(continued on next page)

For crust, preheat oven to 350° F (175° C). Crush graham wafers with a rolling pin or pulse in a food processor to make crumbs. In a mixing bowl, combine graham wafer crumbs, butter and lemon zest. Pat mixture evenly into a 10 in (25 cm) pie plate (see Tip). Bake in oven 10 minutes. Cool to room temperature. Cover and chill in refrigerator until ready to fill. Crust can be made a day in advance.

For filling, combine cream cheese, icing sugar and a generous squeeze of lemon juice in a food processor. Mix until smooth and creamy. Transfer into a large mixing bowl.

In a small bowl, beat whipping cream until light and fluffy, and fold into cream cheese mixture. Gently fill chilled graham crust with creamy filling and chill for at least 3 hours before serving.

For topping, gently heat apple jelly until just warm in a small saucepan. In a medium bowl, pour warm jelly over strawberries and mix lightly. Arrange glazed strawberries on top of cheesecake.

Tip

You can use the bottom of a small glass to help press the graham wafer crumbs evenly into the pie plate.

Topping

1 x 8 oz (250 mL) jar of apple jelly

1 lb (500 g) strawberries, whole, washed and stemmed

Rhubarb Pie with a Meringue Crust

Serves 6

For early pioneers, the robust and hardy rhubarb plant supplied essential vitamins and minerals in spring before any berries ripened. Patches of rhubarb can still be found throughout the Prairie landscape where no trace of a farmhouse remains. Indigenous to Asia, rhubarb was first brought to Europe for its medicinal qualities. Marco Polo had a keen interest in rhubarb, and plantings were recorded in Italy as early as 1608. Huge plantations were soon established in Oxfordshire and Bedfordshire, England, where they still grow today. Officially recognized in Europe as a food by the 17th century, rhubarb was known as "pie plant" because it was most often presented as a pie filling and in other desserts. The English brought the first rhubarb to Canada. This recipe offers a nice balance between the tart rhubarb and the sweet meringue crust.

1 cup (250 mL) sugar

3 Tbsp (45 mL) flour

1 tsp (5 mL) cinnamon

2 lbs (1 kg) rhubarb, frozen or fresh

Meringue

⅓ cup (75 mL) sugar

1 Tbsp (15 mL) cornstarch

5 egg whites

½ tsp (2 mL) cream of tartar

1 x 9 in (23 cm) pie crust, prebaked (or see p. 75 for Great Pie Crust)

Mix sugar, flour and cinnamon in a large bowl. Slice rhubarb into 1 in (2.5 cm) pieces and add to flour–sugar mixture and mix until well coated. In a saucepan over medium heat, cook rhubarb until it is soft and thickened, about 10 minutes. Let cool for at least 30 minutes.

For meringue, mix sugar and cornstarch in a small bowl. In another bowl, with an electric mixer, beat egg whites until foamy. Add cream of tartar and beat in sugar–cornstarch mixture 1 Tbsp (15 mL) at a time until egg whites are stiff and glossy.

Pour cooled rhubarb filling into prepared pie crust and spoon meringue gently on top. Bake meringue-topped pie at 350° F (175° C) for 10 to 12 minutes, until meringue is slightly golden.

🌀 *Don't eat the leaves of the rhubarb plant—they're poisonous.*

🌀 *A member of the buckwheat family, rhubarb is closely related to sorrel. Although rhubarb is technically a vegetable, the stems are used as a fruit in most recipes.*

Cucumber and Fresh Dill Salad

Serves 6 as a side dish

Across the Prairies, cucumbers are ready for harvest starting in July through to around September. The cucumber *(Cucumis sativa)* was first cultivated in India over 3000 years ago. Cucumbers are members of the squash family, which, along with corn and beans, formed the "Three Sisters" of early Native American cuisine. In 1535 Jacques Cartier found "very great cucumbers" growing in what is now Montréal. Because cucumbers are 95% water, they are not especially nutritionally dense, but they are a good source of vitamins C and K, silica and potassium. This water-rich refreshing fruit can also be enjoyed in the heat of summer to keep you feeling as "cool as a cucumber." Fresh dill is available year-round in most supermarkets. For summer use, you can easily grow both dill and cucumbers in your garden.

4 large, long English cucumbers

1 medium red onion, halved and thinly sliced

1 bunch fresh dill, finely chopped, about 1 cup (250 mL)

Dressing
¼ cup (60 mL) cider vinegar

1 to 2 Tbsp (15 to 30 mL) honey, to taste

1 cup (250 mL) sour cream or plain yogurt

sea salt and freshly ground pepper to taste

Wash cucumbers and peel in lengthwise strips, being sure to leave a bit of dark green skin between each strip. Thinly slice, and place slices, along with onion and fresh dill, in a large glass bowl.

For dressing, combine vinegar, honey, sour cream and salt and pepper in a separate small bowl. Add dressing to large bowl and mix well to combine.

Allow salad to sit for at least 15 minutes before serving.

A mature cucumber plant can take up to 1 to 1½ gallons (4 to 5 L) of water per day.

Although considered a vegetable, cucumbers are actually the fruit of the cucumber plant, which belongs to the same family of plants as melons and pumpkins.

Apple and Quinoa Salad

Serves 6 as a main-course salad

Known as the Mother Grain by the Incas, quinoa is not a grain at all but rather a seed from a plant in the same family as spinach and buckwheat. Each seed is covered with saponin, a bitter natural residue that turns soapy in water and acts as a natural pesticide. Quinoa is higher in protein than any other grain; the United Nations has even classified it as a supercrop because it is such a complete foodstuff. Quinoa is available in the grain section of large grocery stores and health food stores across the Prairies. It is grown throughout the Prairie provinces, particularly in Saskatchewan and Manitoba. The Northern Quinoa Corportation is based in Kamsack, Saskatchewan, and that province alone grows around 1600 acres (650 hectares) of quinoa a year.

juice from 1 lemon

1/3 cup (75 mL) apple cider vinegar

1/2 cup (125 mL) orange juice

1/3 cup (75 mL) canola or sunflower oil

1/3 cup (75 mL) honey

5 cups (1.25 L) cooked quinoa (see Tip)

2 apples, cored and chopped

1 bell pepper, diced small

1 cup (250 mL) fresh corn kernels

1/2 cup (125 mL) dried cranberries

1/2 cup (125 mL) currants

1 small red onion, finely chopped

1 cup (250 mL) toasted, chopped pecans

1 cup (250 mL) fresh parsley and mint, chopped

sea salt and freshly ground pepper to taste

Place lemon juice, apple cider vinegar, orange juice, oil and honey in a small bowl and stir to combine.

In a large bowl, combine quinoa and all remaining ingredients, then stir in dressing. Adjust seasonings and refrigerate until ready to serve.

Tip

To cook quinoa, bring 4 cups (1 L) water to a boil in a wide-bottomed pot with a lid. Add a pinch of salt and stir in 2 cups (500 mL) quinoa. Reduce heat to a simmer and cover, and cook until all the water is absorbed, about 25 minutes. You can cook any amount of quinoa you like as long as you keep the 2:1 ratio of liquid to grain. It is also worth experimenting with other liquids such as stock or coconut milk.

If there is any leftover quinoa (or if you want to cook some extra), you can warm it up and add a little cinnamon and cream for a nice breakfast.

Highwood Crossing Canola, Tomato and Tempura Bocconcini Salad

Serves 4

In the Prairies, canola (*Brassica napus*) is known as liquid gold—and for good reason. It stains summer fields across the region with a blanket of yellow, and is the second or third most important crop throughout the Prairie provinces. A distinctly Canadian invention with its home base in Alberta, this member of the cabbage family was developed from rapeseed as a healthier source of vegetable oil in the 1970s. Some 80% of canola grown in the Prairies today has been genetically modified. One source of non-GMO canola is Highwood Crossing, an organic farm in southern Alberta. The farm is the product of the hard work and dedication of the Marshall family, who grow and process everything on their farm to ensure the highest quality. The Marshalls proudly proclaim their cold-pressed organic canola oil to be "Canada's olive oil." It has a fatty acid profile very similar to that of extra virgin olive oil, with all the healthy omega-3 and omega-6 we need for a good diet.

peanut oil

1 lb (500 g) assorted heirloom tomatoes, sliced into thick rounds

handful of fresh basil

17 oz (500 mL) container mini bocconcini, drained and patted very dry

1 recipe of tempura batter (see p. 142)

Highwood Crossing cold-pressed canola oil

juice of 1 lemon

sea salt and freshly ground pepper

Heat peanut oil in pot or deep fryer to 375° F (190° C). Arrange sliced tomato and basil onto individual plates. Dip bocconcini into tempura batter and fry until golden. Serve tempura bocconcini together with tomato slices, drizzle with canola oil and lemon juice. Season with salt and pepper.

Tip

For deep-frying, peanut oil should be 2 to 3 in (5 to 7.5 cm) deep in pot, or use deep fryer according to the manufacturer's directions.

 *Bocconcini, which means "small mouthfuls" in Italian, are small balls of a type of mozzarella cheese. They are usually sold in containers packed in water or whey.*

Roasted Potato Salad

Serves 6 to 8

Baby potatoes fresh from the garden are one of those special summertime treats. Potatoes are a staple in vegetable gardens across the Prairies, with varieties like "Yukon Gold" and "Irish Cobbler" being popular. This potato salad recipe from the Company's Coming library is the perfect accompaniment for a summer barbecue or picnic. You can serve it while the potatoes are still hot, or cool the potatoes before adding them to the other ingredients.

$1\frac{1}{2}$ lbs (680 g) red baby potatoes, halved

$\frac{1}{3}$ cup (75 mL) olive oil, *divided*

$\frac{1}{2}$ tsp (2 mL) salt, *divided*

sprinkle of pepper

3 Tbsp (45 mL) lemon juice

2 Tbsp (30 mL) chopped fresh parsley

1 Tbsp (15 mL) chopped fresh basil or $\frac{3}{4}$ tsp (4 mL) dried basil

$1\frac{1}{2}$ tsp (7 mL) liquid honey

1 tsp (5 mL) chopped fresh thyme or $\frac{3}{4}$ tsp (1 mL) dried thyme

2 cups (500 mL) grape tomatoes

1 cup (250 mL) thinly sliced radicchio, lightly packed

2 Tbsp (30 mL) capers

3 bacon slices, cooked crisp and crumbled

Toss potatoes, 1 Tbsp (15 mL) olive oil, $\frac{1}{4}$ tsp (1 mL) salt and pepper in a large bowl until coated. Arrange in a single layer on a greased baking sheet with sides. Cook in a 400° F (205° C) oven for about 30 minutes, stirring occasionally, until potatoes are tender.

Whisk $\frac{1}{4}$ cup (60 mL) olive oil, lemon juice, parsley, basil, honey, thyme, $\frac{1}{4}$ tsp (1 mL) salt and pepper in same large bowl.

Add tomatoes, radicchio, capers, bacon and potatoes. Stir.

Radicchio is a maroon-coloured salad leaf similar to chicory.

Capers are actually the flower buds from a shrub native to the Mediterranean and parts of Asia. Once these buds are picked, they are sun-dried and then pickled in brine. Capers should always be rinsed and drained prior to use to remove any excess salt.

Grilled Beef Tenderloin with Sautéed Chanterelles

Serves 4

The Canadian cattle industry began in the 1850s in what is now British Columbia and made its way into the southeastern foothills of Alberta in the 1870s, when the North-West Mounted Police arrived to sweep the American whiskey traders out of the West. The southern Prairies are a naturally suitable climate for ranching, with its many streams, sheltered valleys and Chinook winds. Today, the cattle industry is huge—it contributes over 15 billion dollars annually to Canada's economy, and the Prairie provinces are key players. What could be better than Canadian Prairie beef cooked on a barbecue on a hot summer day!

Mushrooms

1 to 2 Tbsp (15 to 30 mL) olive oil

3 shallots, sliced

1 lb (500 g) fresh chanterelles

1 clove garlic, minced

½ cup (125 mL) white wine

1 cup (250 mL) parsley, chopped

¼ cup (60 mL) chives, chopped

sea salt and freshly ground black pepper

4 x 6 oz (170 g) beef tenderloin medallions

olive oil, for brushing

2 tsp (10 mL) kosher salt

freshly ground black pepper

Remove beef medallions from refrigerator 15 minutes before cooking.

To prepare mushrooms, heat olive oil in a skillet over medium-high heat and sauté shallots until soft. Add chanterelles and garlic and continue to sauté for 5 to 7 minutes, then add white wine and cook until liquid evaporates. Remove from heat and stir in parsley and chives. Season with salt and pepper.

Prepare a grill or a stove-top grill pan to medium-high heat. Brush beef lightly with olive oil and season with salt and pepper. Place on grill and cook, without moving it, until nice grill marks appear, about 4 minutes. Turn medallions and continue to grill until medium-rare, about 3 to 4 minutes more. Set aside on a cutting board to rest for 5 minutes before serving. Divide medallions among plates and spoon on mushrooms.

Loveday Mushroom Farms, in Winnipeg, Manitoba, produces a wide range of mushrooms, including white, portobella, shiitake and enoki. You can experiment with different types of mushrooms in this recipe.

Alberta Beef Burgers

Serves 4

Did you know that almost one half of all Canadian beef comes from Alberta? Sunshine Organic Farm, near Warburg, Alberta, raises certified organic beef that are fed only organically grown feed and are grass-finished. Grass-fed beef are high in healthful omega-3 fatty acids. Hamburgers of all types are beloved throughout the Prairies, but the hamburger itself actually has international origins. It originated in Hamburg, Germany—sort of. There was no bun, no ketchup and no drive-through; it was just a ground-meat steak known as "Hamburg Steak." Many claim to have invented the modern burger, but it is generally agreed that the burger first reached wide exposure during the St. Louis World's Fair in 1904.

1½ lbs (680 g) ground beef

1 large egg

1 Tbsp (15 mL) grainy Dijon mustard

⅓ cup (75 mL) fine breadcrumbs

sea salt and freshly ground pepper

Preheat grill to high. Mix all ingredients together and form into 4 thick patties; thick patties make juicy burgers.

Grill patties, turning once, for 4 to 6 minutes per side, until internal temperature reaches 160° F (71° C). Serve patties on toasted buns with your favourite accompaniments.

Tip

For a better burger...

• Handling the meat lightly when mixing and shaping will help prevent it from turning into a hockey puck.

• Make sure the grill is hot to seal in the juices and keep the meat from sticking.

• When shaping your patties, sneak a piece of your favourite cheese (e.g., Bleu, Brie or Cheddar) in the centre, making sure it is completely surrounded by the meat, for a volcanic cheeseburger.

Here are some food safety tips when handling raw meat:

- *Store it in the refrigerator and use it within 2 days, or freeze it.*

- *Wash your hands and everything the meat contacted with a solution of 1 tsp (5 mL) unscented bleach per litre of water.*

- *Do not place the cooked burgers on the same surface the raw meat was on.*

- *Cook ground meat until it reaches 160° F (71° C) in temperature.* E. coli *is of particular concern for children, the elderly or anyone with a compromised immune system.*

Lemongrass Pork

Serves 4

A favourite recipe from Jean Paré, this Vietnamese main dish features pleasing contrasts of subtle lemongrass, sharp chili and beautiful colours served atop a bed of rice vermicelli. Pork from the Prairie provinces is a lean meat choice. The Manitoba Pork Council has recently partnered with a number of sporting organizations, including the Winnipeg Jets, to promote the nutrient-rich and healthful pork produced in the province.

8 oz (225 mL) rice vermicelli

boiling water, to cover

1 Tbsp (15 mL) canola oil

1 medium onion, halved lengthwise and thinly sliced crosswise

2 cloves garlic, minced, or ¹⁄₂ tsp (2 mL) garlic powder

1 lb (500 g) boneless pork loin, cut into 1 in (1.25 cm) thick slices

1 stalk of lemongrass

2 Tbsp (30 mL) chili sauce

1¹⁄₂ Tbsp (25 mL) fish sauce

1 tsp (5 mL) sugar

dash of cayenne pepper (optional)

2 Tbsp (30 mL) thinly sliced green onion

¹⁄₄ cup (60 mL) julienned carrot

¹⁄₄ cup (60 mL) thinly slivered red pepper

cilantro sprigs for garnish

Cover vermicelli with boiling water in a small bowl. Let stand for 2 minutes. Drain.

Heat a wok or frying pan on medium-high until hot. Add canola oil. Add onion and garlic. Stir-fry for 2 minutes. Transfer to a medium bowl. Add ½ of pork slices to hot wok. Stir-fry for 2 to 3 minutes until no longer pink. Add to onion mixture. Stir-fry remaining pork until no longer pink. Leave in wok.

Remove outer leaves and rough tops of lemongrass, leaving 3 to 4 in (7.5 to 10 cm) root. Place on cutting surface. Press root with flat of knife. Chop finely. Add to pork in wok. Add chili sauce, fish sauce, sugar and cayenne pepper. Stir. Add onion mixture and any juices. Stir-fry for about 2 minutes until pork is coated and sauce is slightly thickened. Makes 3 cups (750 mL) pork mixture. Place 1 cup (250 mL) vermicelli in each of 4 individual bowls. Divide and spoon pork mixture over vermicelli.

Arrange green onion, carrot and red pepper over pork mixture. Garnish with cilantro.

Unsurprisingly, lemongrass has a decidedly lemony flavour—it contains an essential oil that's also found in lemon peel. The lemongrass plant is a tall, woody grass that looks a little like a very large green onion. Only the bottom 10 cm (4 in) of the stem is eaten. Remove the tough outer layers and bruise with the blunt edge of a knife before chopping. The upper portion of the lemongrass is too tough to eat, but can be used to add flavour to custards and poaching liquids or to skewer shish kabobs. If you can't find fresh lemongrass, try dried—just remember that 1 tsp (5 mL) is equal to one stalk of lemongrass.

Mu Shu Duck with Peaches and Daikon

Serves 4

Game hunting is a popular fall pastime in the rural Prairies, especially hunting for geese, wild turkey, prairie chicken, partridge, grouse and duck. These game birds were an important food source for Canada's indigenous peoples, and have always been abundant through the Prairies, at least seasonally; probably the best-known duck; the mallard (*Anas platyrhynchos*), is also the most common duck here. If you don't want to hunt for duck yourself, you can buy it at most grocery stores and specialty grocers.

Duck

8 oz (250 g) duck breast, about 2 breasts, cut into strips

¼ cup (60 mL) rice vinegar, *divided*

2 Tbsp (30 mL) soy sauce

1 tsp (5 mL) sesame oil

1 Tbsp (15 mL) garlic, minced

1 Tbsp (15 mL) fresh ginger, finely chopped

Daikon

1 x 4 in (10 cm) daikon radish, grated

½ tsp (2 mL) sugar

1 Tbsp (15 mL) + ½ cup (125 mL) green onion, finely sliced

(continued on next page)

In a bowl, toss duck with 3 Tbsp (45 mL) rice vinegar, soy sauce, sesame oil, garlic and ginger. Cover and marinate, refrigerated, for 2 hours.

In another bowl, toss daikon with 1 Tbsp (15 mL) rice vinegar, sugar and 1 Tbsp (15 mL) green onion. Set aside.

Heat a splash of oil in a wok (or heavy-bottomed pan) and add marinated duck strips. Stir-fry over high heat until browned and cooked through, about 3 minutes. Remove from the pan, toss with ½ cup (125 mL) green onion and set aside.

Reduce heat to medium and cook peaches in wok for 5 minutes, then set aside. Add a splash of oil to wok and cook eggs, sunny side up.

Serve duck, daikon, peaches, eggs and enoki mushrooms on a platter along with side serving plates. Spread a spoonful of hoisin sauce on a flatbread and add your toppings. Roll up and enjoy.

The world's largest mallard duck statue, with a wingspan of 25 feet (7.6 metres), is located a short drive northeast of Edmonton in the village of Andrew.

grape seed oil or canola oil for stir frying

2 fresh peaches, cut into eighths

4 large eggs

4 oz (125 g) fresh enoki mushrooms

hoisin sauce

1 package store-bought flatbread, such as chapatti

Wild Salmon en Papillote

Serves 4

Although it is not found in Prairie waters, salmon is our most popular seafood choice. We can purchase it from local retailers year-round, but the time to really indulge is during salmon season, which runs from June through September. Wild salmon is always the best choice, even if it costs a bit more, because you get a tastier, leaner and more natural fish. There are five species of wild salmon found in the Pacific: sockeye, pink, chum, chinook, steelhead and coho. Sockeye is the most sought-after salmon variety because of its oil content and rich colour, believed to come from a diet high in shrimp. But many of us don't just sit around and wait for this tasty fish to come to the local market—we love to take off to coastal British Columbia for a week's respite, book a salmon fishing charter and stock up on our favourite fish for winter.

4 wild salmon fillets

4 leeks, white parts only, thinly sliced and well washed

¼ cup (60 mL) dry white wine

sea salt and freshly ground pepper

1 bunch dill or other fresh herb, chopped

¼ cup (60 mL) unsalted butter, cut into 4 pieces

1 egg white, lightly beaten

1 lemon, sliced

sautéed vegetables (optional)

Heat oven to 350° F (175° C). Fold a 24 in (60 cm) sheet of parchment paper in half, and cut out a heart shape about 4 in (10 cm) larger than a fish fillet. Place fillet near fold, and place a handful of leeks next to it. Sprinkle with wine, salt, pepper and dill and top with a piece of butter. Brush edges of parchment paper with egg white, fold paper to enclose fish, and make small overlapping folds to seal edges, starting at curve of heart. Be sure each fold overlaps the one before it to create an airtight seal. Repeat with rest of fillets. Put packages on a baking sheet, and bake until paper is puffed and brown, about 10 to 15 minutes. Serve salmon in packets with lemon slices and sautéed vegetables. Be careful of steam when opening packets.

The leek is the emblem of Wales, and Welsh people still wear one on their lapel on St. David's Day, March 1.

Cooking in parchment paper, en papillote *in French, is an easy, low-fat way to prepare fish. The word* papillote *is derived from* papillon, *meaning butterfly, and hence, why the parchment pouch is traditionally folded into a heart or butterfly shape. Try cooking vegetables in parchment as well.*

Blackened Trout with Oven-dried Tomatoes

Serves 2

Even though the Prairies are landlocked, we love to eat fresh fish here, including the ever-popular trout. Fresh and frozen trout are available year-round, but Prairie folk most frequently indulge in the coral-fleshed fish during the summer. Dozens of trout farms offer U-fish facilities, fish for stocking home ponds and much more. In addition, wild trout are abundant in our waterways. These wild fish not only taste great, but are great fun to catch—or catch and release if that is what you prefer. Trout have undoubtedly made their mark throughout the Prairies: the bull trout is Alberta's provincial fish, northern Saskatchewan lakes are known for their huge lake trout catches, and Pine River has been named the Rainbow Trout Capital of Manitoba.

2 lbs (1 kg) Roma tomatoes, halved lengthwise

3 cloves garlic, minced

¼ cup (60 mL) fresh thyme, chopped

sea salt and freshly ground black pepper to taste

½ cup (125 mL) extra virgin olive oil

Spice Mixture

2 tsp (10 mL) paprika

2 tsp (10 mL) chipotle powder or chili powder

2 tsp (10 mL) ground cumin

2 tsp (10 mL) dried thyme

1 tsp (5 mL) freshly ground black pepper

1 tsp (5 mL) sea salt

2 fresh trout, gutted but whole

2 Tbsp (30 mL) canola oil

Preheat oven to 250° F (120° C). Scoop out seeds from tomatoes. Mix garlic with thyme, salt and pepper and olive oil. Place tomatoes cut-side up in a roasting pan and drizzle with garlic mixture. Bake for at least 3 hours or until tomatoes are dehydrated but still chewy.

Mix all spices together in a bowl.

Rinse trout with water and pat dry with paper towels. Brush canola oil on trout and rub spice mixture all over. Heat a heavy-bottomed skillet until it is smoking hot. Place prepared trout in skillet and cook for 2 to 4 minutes and turn over. Cook until trout is firm and cooked through, 3 to 4 minutes. Fish should flake easily with a fork but should not be dry. Serve with oven-dried tomatoes on side.

Tip

Oven-drying tomatoes is a great way to preserve these tasty bits of summer sunshine. Grow tomatoes in your garden or in containers, or pick them up at farmers' markets.

Tip

Any leftover tomatoes can be covered in olive oil and stored in a jar. They will keep for up to 3 weeks refrigerated.

Summer Squash Ratatouille

Serves 4 as a main course, 6 as a side dish

The difference between summer squash and winter squash is in their shelf life. Winter squash, such as pumpkins, develop hard rinds and can be stored for months, whereas summer squash, such as zucchini, are best eaten before they mature and develop a bitter flavour. You can grow both types in your garden, and squash grows well in the Prairies, so you will need many delicious recipes to use them all up. Most squash are ready in about 50 days from sowing to harvest. Early Native peoples in North and South America discovered that members of the squash family *(Cucurbitacae)* love to cross-pollinate, giving them abundant and interesting varieties to choose from. Grown as part of their "Three Sisters" Diet along with corn and beans, squash was crossbread in hopes of producing larger seeds and flesh that was less bitter.

1 medium eggplant, 2½ lbs (1.2 kg), cut into ½ in (1.25 cm) cubes

olive oil for cooking

1 lb (500 g) assorted summer squash, as much variety as possible, cut into ½ in (1.25 cm) cubes

2 medium onions, sliced

2 red bell peppers, seeded and cut into ½ in (1.25 cm) strips

3 ripe but firm tomatoes, about 1 lb (500 g), seeded and quartered

2 cloves garlic, minced

⅓ cup (75 mL) mixture of chopped fresh rosemary, thyme, basil, fennel and marjoram

pinch of dried lavender

sea salt and freshly ground black pepper to taste

crusty French bread

Lay eggplant cubes on paper towels and sprinkle with salt. Let them sit for 15 minutes, then rinse and pat dry. Have a large bowl ready. Heat a splash of olive oil in a large skillet or casserole over medium heat. Add eggplant chunks and cook until they start to soften. Remove from skillet and set aside in bowl to make room for next vegetable. Add more olive oil as needed, and continue with squash, onions and peppers separately.

Return all vegetables to pan; add tomatoes, garlic and herbs. Season with salt and pepper and stir to mix. Simmer over medium heat until much of liquid is evaporated, about 10 minutes, then cover, turn heat to medium low and cook until vegetables are tender, about 45 minutes to 1 hour, stirring occasionally to prevent sticking. Serve at room temperature with French bread.

Ratatouille is a dish from the Provençal region of southern France. It's also good cold, if there are leftovers.

Squash blossoms are also edible and make a great vessel for stuffing and deep frying. Make sure you choose the male stems (but leave a few for pollination) and leave the fruit-bearing females for an abundant summer supply.

Char-grilled Taber Corn with Jalapeño Lime Butter

Serves 6

Taber is the Corn Capital of Canada and proud home to the annual Cornfest in August. Taber receives more sunlight during the year than any other region in Canada, and its hot summer days and cooler nights provide optimal conditions for bringing up the sugar content in corn. As a result of its climate, soil type and use of irrigation, the Taber area is renowned for growing the sweetest corn. Corn *(Zea mays)* is native to the Americas, and its history dates back thousands of years. The first corn was probably a popcorn variety, and it wasn't until its introduction to the European settlers that sweet corn strains started to emerge. Sadly, in the quest for sweet corn, we have lost many of the hundreds of varieties that were once common. Corn is really a grain, though we generally eat it fresh, as a vegetable.

6 ears of Taber corn

Jalapeño Lime Butter

1 cup (250 mL) unsalted butter, softened

1 jalapeño pepper, seeded and finely chopped (see Tip)

zest from 1 lime

1 clove garlic, minced

1 tsp (5 mL) sea salt

lime wedges

sea salt to taste

Preheat barbecue to medium-high heat. Peel back husks, leaving them attached, and remove silk from corn. Rewrap, tying with butcher twine or kitchen string if necessary. Barbecue for about 10 minutes, turning to cook all sides. If husks start to burn, spritz with water.

For Jalapeño Lime Butter, mix ingredients together in a bowl or in a food processor. Wrap in plastic and shape into a cylinder about 1 in (2.5 cm) in diameter, and refrigerate.

Serve hot corn with rounds of Jalapeño Lime Butter, lime wedges and sea salt.

Tip

To keep the sugars from turning to starch, keep freshly picked corn as cool as possible and enjoy it soon after harvesting. Fresh corn can be steamed, boiled or grilled, and older corn can be cut from the cob and added to soups and stews.

Tip

Hot peppers contain capsaicin in the seeds and ribs. Removing the seeds and ribs will reduce the heat. Wear rubber gloves when handling hot peppers and avoid touching your eyes. Wash your hands well afterwards.

Praline Pecans, Beets and Blue Cheese on Baby Greens

Serves 4

Beets are a wonderfully versatile root vegetable. Many people don't know that the top leafy part of the beet plant is also edible—beet tops are similar to spinach or Swiss chard. If you don't like the way that red beets stain your hands and work surface, try looking for chiogga (or candy cane), purple or golden varieties at local farmers' markets across the Prairie provinces; these beets also have a sweeter and more mellow flavour than most dark red types. The candied pecans, blue cheese and citrus and Dijon dressing all contribute to the sophisticated and distinguished flavour combination in this summer salad from the Company's Coming collection.

1 medium fresh beet, scrubbed clean (see Tip)

2 tsp (10 mL) butter

1/4 cup (60 mL) brown sugar, lightly packed

3/4 cup (175 mL) pecan halves

1/4 cup (60 mL) orange juice

2 Tbsp (30 mL) chopped fresh chives

2 Tbsp (30 mL) olive oil

2 Tbsp (30 mL) white wine vinegar

1 Tbsp (15 mL) Dijon mustard

1/8 tsp (0.5 mL) pepper

1 1/2 cups (375 mL) mixed baby greens (lightly packed)

1/2 cup (125 mL) crumbled blue (or goat) cheese

Microwave beet, covered, for about 4 minutes until tender. Let stand until cool. Peel and cut into 1/4 in (6 mm) wedges (see Tip).

Heat and stir butter and brown sugar in a frying pan until sugar is dissolved. Stir in pecans. Spread on a baking sheet lined with greased foil. Bake in a 375° F (190° C) oven for about 8 minutes, stirring once, until browned. Transfer to cutting board. Let stand until cool, then chop.

Whisk orange juice, chives, olive oil, vinegar, mustard and pepper together.

Arrange greens in centre of a serving plate. Arrange beet wedges around greens. Sprinkle with cheese and pecans and drizzle with dressing.

Tip

Wear gloves when cutting fresh beets to avoid staining your hands. It is also easier to peel beets after they have been microwaved or roasted—the skins will slip off quite easily.

Tip

Instead of microwaving your beet, you can roast it in the oven. Wrap the beet in foil and bake in a 375° F (190° C) oven for about 1½ hours until tender. Remove and discard the foil and let the beet cool before peeling.

Iced Tea with Fresh Mint

Serves 4

Across the Prairies, there are at least 75 tearooms that serve a variety of teas, both iced and hot. Although we love our coffee, tea is gaining popularity as we strive for a healthier lifestyle, and sipping afternoon tea at the local teahouse is becoming a favourite pastime. Traditionally, iced tea was served as a refreshing punch spiked with alcohol. The version we think of most often today, a freshly brewed tea sweetened and flavoured with lemon, first became popular after being served at the 1904 St. Louis World's Fair. Iced tea can be made with any tea you like, from the standard black tea to green tea and even caffeine-free herbal tea and rooibos.

6 cups (1.5 L) cold water

5 level tsp (25 mL) good quality, loose tea

⅔ cup (150 mL) white sugar, or to taste

1 handful of fresh mint, rinsed and patted dry

1 lime or lemon

Bring 4 cups (1 L) of water to a boil. Place tea in a pitcher and pour boiling water over tea. Let infuse for 30 minutes.

Stir in sugar to dissolve and strain tea into a clean pitcher. Add remaining water.

Bruise mint by crushing it lightly with a rolling pin or the bottom of a glass and place in pitcher.

Chill tea for at least 1 hour. Remove mint before serving, and serve with a wedge of lime or lemon and a sprig of mint, if desired.

There are two traditional types of iced tea—sweetened and unsweetened. Our general preference in the Prairies seems to be the sweetened variety. Beyond the traditional black tea, you can make iced tea using rooibos tea from South Africa, green teas from China, chai from India or even matcha from Japan.

Some people call the alcohol-spiked version of iced tea "iced tea on a stick." Iced coffee is also a popular summer drink available homemade or purchased from fine coffee shops throughout the province.

Saskatoon Pie

Serves 6

People who grew up in the Prairies, particularly Saskatchewan, have fond memories of secret saskatoon patches and the bountiful harvests that lasted all winter long. Saskatchewan produces over a third of Canada's saskatoon crop. The saskatoon (*Amelanchier alnifolia*, also called serviceberry and juneberry), which is related to cherries and apples, is also an essential winter food for wildlife. Although most prolific on the Prairies, the saskatoon grows from coast to coast and is a truly Canadian berry, but to many Eastern Canadians, it remains a mystery. Interior B.C. and Plains First Nations peoples, however, have been enjoying them for centuries in everything from pemmican to porridge and, of course, freshly picked. The name *saskatoon* is believed to be a shortened form of the Cree or Blackfoot name for this berry. In Britain, saskatoons were pulled off the shelves in June 2004 after their safety was questioned because there was no history of people eating the berries in Europe!

pastry, enough for a double crust (see opposite, or use purchased)

1 egg white, beaten, for brushing pastry

6 cups (1.5 L) fresh saskatoons

¼ cup (60 mL) cornstarch

1 cup (250 mL) unbleached sugar

juice of ⅓ lemon

pinch of sea salt

1 Tbsp (15 mL) unsalted butter

2 Tbsp (30 mL) heavy cream (32%), for top of crust

¼ cup (60 mL) unbleached sugar, for top of crust

Preheat oven to 400° F (200° C). Roll pastry out and use 1 to line a pie plate. Brush inside of bottom crust with egg white to prevent juices from soaking in and making it soggy. Pick over saskatoons and toss together in a large bowl with cornstarch, sugar, lemon juice and salt. Pour into crust and dot with butter. Secure top crust, and be sure to cut air vents. Brush with cream and sprinkle with sugar. Bake for 12 minutes. Turn heat down to 365° F (185° C) and bake 20 to 30 minutes until crust is golden brown and filling is bubbly. Place on a wire rack to cool for at least 1 hour.

Tip

For individual free-form pies, as shown at right, simply divide pastry into 6 equal portions, roll out to ⅛ in (3 mm) and lay out on a baking sheet lined with parchment paper. Brush with egg white and divide filling evenly onto rounds, leaving a 1 in (2.5 cm) border. Fold border up over filling, leaving centre open. Dot fruit with butter, brush pastry with cream and sprinkle with sugar. Follow baking instructions as above, reducing baking time to about 15 minutes.

Great Pie Crust

Mix flour, salt and sugar in a bowl. Using a cheese grater, grate frozen butter into flour mixture. Toss lightly to distribute butter and add lemon juice and enough water for dough just to come together. Divide in half, wrap each piece in plastic wrap and flatten into a disc. Chill for at least 30 minutes before using. Makes enough for a double-crusted pie.

Great Pie Crust

2½ cups (625 mL) flour

1 tsp (5 mL) sea salt

1 Tbsp (15 mL) sugar

1 cup (250 mL) unsalted butter, frozen

1 Tbsp (15 mL) lemon juice

about ⅓ cup (75 mL) ice water

Currant Cooler

Serves 2

Currants are members of the genus *Ribes,* which includes the edible currants (black currant, red currant and white currant) along with gooseberries and many ornamental plants. They are native to the temperate regions of the Northern Hemisphere and grow well throughout the Prairies. Black currants are the most popular variety grown here, and can be found from southern Alberta through to Manitoba. Black currants produce more juice per hectare than oranges and are also higher in vitamin C. Currants are at their peak in August and are available at many U-pick farms. They also make a beautiful fruit-bearing shrub for any yard, and often can be found in the wild.

ice

6 oz (170 mL) currant juice

4 oz (115 mL) vodka

3 drops dry vermouth

frozen currants for garnish

Fill cocktail shaker ½ full of ice. Pour in currant juice, vodka and dry vermouth. Shake and strain. Pour into martini glasses and garnish with frozen currants.

Historically, currants have been used in many jams, jellies and drinks—for example, currants were boiled to make tea.

Vodka is best kept in the freezer, so it's ready for use in your favourite cocktails.

Raspberry Tart

Serves 6 to 8

Fragrantly sweet and subtly tart, raspberries (*Rubus* spp.) are a favourite Prairie fruit. A member of the rose family, raspberries can be grown anywhere in the Prairies, although it is slightly more difficult to grow them in the Chinook belt of southern Alberta. The wild raspberry *(R. idaeus)* occurs naturally in thickets, open woods, fields and on rocky hillsides across the Prairie provinces and produces a smaller but equally delicious berry. Raspberries are healthy, antioxidant-rich berries, high in ellagic acid—the same family of tannins that make wine, green tea and fruit, such as pomegranates, an important part of a healthy lifestyle. Raspberries are also an excellent source of manganese, vitamin C and dietary fibre, and the leaves make a soothing herbal tea.

Crust

1¼ cups (310 mL)
all-purpose flour

¼ cup (60 mL) sugar

½ cup (125 mL) or 1 stick
unsalted butter, cold and
cut into pieces

2 to 3 Tbsp (30 to 45 mL)
cold water

Filling

2 x 8 oz (250 g) containers
mascarpone, room
temperature

½ cup (125 mL) sugar

1 tsp (5 mL) vanilla

3 cups (750 mL)
raspberries, picked over

Glaze

1 x 8 oz (250 mL) jar of
apple jelly

For crust, place flour, sugar and butter in a food processor and blend until mixture resembles coarse meal. Add 2 Tbsp (30 mL) of water until incorporated. Add enough remaining water, if necessary, until mixture comes together but is still crumbly. Wrap dough in plastic and refrigerate for 1 hour.

Preheat oven to 350° F (175° C). Press crust mixture evenly onto bottom and sides of an 11 in (28 cm) tart pan with removable fluted rim or 6 to 8 individual tart tins. Prick crust with a fork, line it with parchment and weigh it down with pie weights or dried beans. Bake in middle of oven until golden, about 15 minutes. Let cool to room temperature and chill for 1 hour in refrigerator.

Make filling while the crust chills. In a bowl, using an electric mixer, beat mascarpone, sugar and vanilla together until smooth. Pour filling into chilled crust, spreading evenly, and arrange raspberries on top.

If keeping tart longer than one day, brush raspberries lightly with a glaze of warmed apple jelly.

Tip

When out picking raspberries in your yard or favourite U-pick farm, be sure to keep them as cool as possible, and store them unwashed. Ideally, pick them during cooler times of the day or on a cloudy day.

Mascarpone is a rich cream cheese that has the consistency of a stiff whipped cream. Originally produced in the Lombardy region of Italy, it is now available in grocery stores and Italian markets.

Blueberry Ice Cream

Makes 4 cups (1 L)

Blueberries, which grow across much of the country, were a significant food source for Canada's Native peoples, and parts of the plant were also important in medical uses. About half of Canada's commercial blueberry harvest comes from cultivated highbush varieties (*Vaccinium corymbosum*), and the rest is supplied by managed stands of wild lowbush berries (*V. angustifolium and V. myrtilloides*). Several varieties of wild blueberries grow in bogs and forests throughout the Prairie provinces. "Wild blues" are smaller, with a deeper blue colour and more intense blueberry flavour than the cultivated berries. Canada is the world's largest supplier of lowbush blueberries.

1 cup (250 mL) whole milk (3%)

3 cups (750 mL) heavy cream (32%)

1 vanilla bean, split lengthwise

5 egg yolks

¾ cup (175 mL) sugar

2½ cups (625 mL) washed blueberries

In a heavy-bottomed saucepan, heat milk, cream and vanilla bean until just before boiling, stirring occasionally. Remove from heat. Take out vanilla bean and scrape out seeds, adding them to milk. Set aside.

In a mixing bowl, whisk egg yolks and sugar until pale yellow and thickened. Slowly pour about 1 cup (250 mL) of hot mixture into egg yolks, whisking constantly. Add yolk mixture back into rest of cream and cook over medium heat, stirring constantly, until mixture thickens and coats back of a spoon. Be sure not to let mixture boil at any time or it will curdle. Pour through a fine strainer into a bowl, add blueberries and freeze in an ice cream maker according to manufacturer's instructions.

Bursting with flavour, full of antioxidants and containing very few calories, blueberries are said to be among the healthiest of foods and are considered a superfood.

Many adults fondly remember the ice cream sold by vendors travelling the streets of their neighbourhoods during long, hot summer days of their childhood. Even today when the familiar music is heard wafting through open windows, it makes us all want to "scream for ice cream."

Tiramisu

Serves 9

Although Italians didn't immigrate to the Canadian Prairies in the same numbers as other Europeans (such as Ukrainians) did, many did make their way across the Prairies, and set up close-knit community groups and organizations. Edmonton, for example, boasts a Little Italy community, where you can find the Italian Centre Shop, which was founded in 1959 by Franco (Frank) Spinelli, who immigrated to Canada in 1951. The Italian Centre has gone on to become a cultural focal point for the Italian community, and a great source of fresh produce and Italian and European products. The marsala wine in this delicious, creamy and simple tiramisu is a typical Italian ingredient.

1 cup (250 mL) whipping cream

2 cups (500 mL) mascarpone cheese

⅓ cup (75 mL) + 2 Tbsp (30 mL) sugar

¼ cup (60 mL) marsala wine, *divided*

½ cup (125 mL) cold strong prepared coffee

24 ladyfingers (approximately)

1 Tbsp (15 mL) cocoa

Beat whipping cream in small bowl until soft peaks form. Using same beaters, beat mascarpone cheese, ⅓ cup (75 mL) sugar and 1 Tbsp (15 mL) marsala wine in medium bowl until smooth. Fold in whipped cream.

Stir coffee, 3 Tbsp (45 mL) marsala wine and 2 Tbsp (30 mL) sugar in small shallow bowl until sugar is dissolved. Quickly dip half of ladyfingers into coffee mixture, 1 at a time, until partially soaked through. Arrange in single layer in ungreased 8 x 8 in (20 x 20 cm) baking dish, trimming to fit if necessary. Spread half of cheese mixture evenly over ladyfingers. Repeat with remaining ladyfingers, coffee mixture and cheese mixture.

Sift cocoa through fine sieve over top. Chill, covered, for at least 4 hours or overnight.

Fresh raspberries make an attractive garnish for this dessert.

You can make this tiramisu alcohol-free by increasing the amount of coffee to replace the marsala wine.

Fruit Smoothie

Serves 1

Berries were an important part of the Plains Natives' lives long before the first Europeans came to the Prairies. Berries were eaten fresh, dried or preserved in oil. They were used for dyes, medicine and even jewellery. Learning to use indigenous foods such as berries often sustained early settlers during their first months in Canada. Today, Saskatchewan has over 350 fruit and berry growers, with saskatoons being the most commonly grown. Alberta has some 300 fruit and berry growers and over 1000 hectares (over 2500 acres) of land devoted to the industry. The most common types of native Prairie berries are saskatoons, raspberries, strawberries, chokecherries and cranberries. New species, such as the honeyberry (*Lonicera kamchatika;* edible honeysuckle) from Siberia, are being introduced regularly, and new winter-hardy varieties of fruits such as cherries are being successfully grown on farms such as S'toons and Stuff near Stonewall, Manitoba.

1 banana, peeled and frozen

¾ cup (175 mL) fresh or frozen berries

¼ cup (60 mL) coconut milk

1 cup (250 mL) vanilla soy milk

1 Tbsp (15 mL) almond butter

¼ cup (60 mL) crushed ice

Purée all ingredients in a blender until smooth.

Tip
Coconut milk from a can will keep in the fridge for 4 to 5 days.

Fruit smoothies are perfect for breakfast or a refreshing snack. Add some flaxseed or bran for a really healthy kick.

Dr. Ieuan Evans is known for his work on breeding and evaluating fruit tree varieties for the Prairies. The Evans Cherry, which has sold some 3 million trees, is named for him.

Manitoba Wild Rice Salad

Serves 6

Wild rice is not actually a type of rice; it is the grain of a grass that grows in marshy areas, and it is the only cereal that is native to Canada. Manitoba is Canada's most active player in wild rice production, growing a quarter of Canada's wild rice. Wild rice is high in protein (twice that of brown rice) and fibre, and is also a good source of potassium and a number of the B vitamins. Unfortunately, wild rice is one of the most expensive types of rice because it does not lend itself to commercial cultivation, and in Canada it is still harvested mostly from wild plants.

2½ cups (625 mL) water

1 tsp (5 mL) salt, *divided*

1 cup (250 mL) wild rice

1 cup (250 mL) diced peeled jicama

1 cup (250 mL) diced unpeeled cooking apple (such as McIntosh)

⅓ cup (75 mL) chopped dried apricot

⅓ cup (75 mL) chopped dried figs

⅓ cup (75 mL) grated carrot

⅓ cup (75 mL) raisins

¼ cup (60 mL) diced red pepper

2 Tbsp (30 mL) sliced green onion

⅔ cup (150 mL) plain yogurt

1 Tbsp (15 mL) lemon juice

1 Tbsp (15 mL) mango chutney, larger pieces chopped

1 tsp (5 mL) hot curry paste

1 Tbsp (15 mL) chopped fresh cilantro or parsley

Combine water and ¼ tsp (1 mL) salt in a medium saucepan. Bring to a boil. Add rice. Stir. Reduce heat to medium-low. Simmer, covered, for about 75 minutes, without stirring, until tender. Drain any remaining liquid. Transfer to large bowl. Cool. Add jicama, apple, apricot, figs, carrot, raisins, red pepper and green onion. Stir.

Stir yogurt, lemon juice, mango chutney, curry paste and ¾ tsp (4 mL) salt in a small bowl until smooth. Add to rice mixture. Stir. Chill, covered, for 1 hour to blend flavours. Sprinkle with cilantro.

Wild rice has a naturally nutty, chewy flavour.

A few hardy varieties of apricot grow on the Prairies, particularly in Saskatchewan and Manitoba. Most Prairie apricot varieties are best used for jam.

Bison Carpaccio Salad

Serves 4 to 6

Bison were the centre of life for the Native peoples of the Prairies, providing everything from nourishment, clothes and medicine to spiritual inspiration. It is commonly estimated that there were 60 million bison on the Prairies, and that the bison spread as far south as Mexico. Within just a few short years in the mid-1880s, the pressures of settlement, agriculture, drought and sport hunting drove the bison almost to extinction, thus threatening the existence of an entire way of life. Many years of hard work and dedication have saved the bison from extinction, and today we can enjoy this highly nutritious and great-tasting meat from farm-raised herds. With thick hair cover to provide protection through winter, the bison is exceptionally well suited to our cool climate—Alberta grows half of Canada's bison, with Manitoba and Saskatchewan coming in second and third with 29% and 10% of the herd, respectively.

1 clove garlic, minced

2 shallots, finely diced

1 Tbsp (15 mL) balsamic vinegar

¼ cup (60 mL) extra virgin olive oil, plus additional for drizzling

1 lb (500 g) bison tenderloin

sea salt and freshly crushed peppercorns

2 Tbsp (30 mL) grainy Dijon mustard

¼ cup (60 mL) chopped fresh parsley

¼ cup (60 mL) chopped fresh dill

3 Tbsp (45 mL) freshly crushed peppercorns

baby salad greens, washed and spun dry (about 2 cups [500 mL]) per person

1 bunch fresh radishes, sliced

fresh chives, thinly sliced

Combine garlic, shallots, balsamic vinegar and olive oil in a bowl. Place tenderloin in a pan and coat evenly with garlic mixture. Let marinate in fridge for 4 to 6 hours.

Remove tenderloin from fridge and pat dry. Season well with sea salt and peppercorns, and sear over high heat (or grill) until nicely brown, about 5 minutes. Remove from heat and let cool. Rub mustard over entire surface of tenderloin and then roll in fresh herbs. Wrap tightly in cellophane and freeze for 3 hours to make slicing much easier.

Slice meat as thinly as possible and serve with salad greens, radishes, chives, a drizzle of olive oil and a sprinkle of sea salt.

Tip

Be sure to allow yourself the 4 to 6 hours needed for the marinating and a further 3 hours for freezing. You can prepare the carpaccio ahead of time by slicing the tenderloin and laying the slices out in a circular pattern in a single layer on individual serving plates, covering well with cellophane and keeping in the freezer up to 5 days. Because the meat is so thinly sliced, it thaws within 5 to 10 minutes. Don't leave it longer than that because, when left too long, it loses its nice red colour.

∾ *This dish is named after Renaissance artist Vittore Carpaccio, whose work often displayed a predilection for red. Carpaccio is most often made using beef, but many foods work well in the style of carpaccio. Ultra-fresh tuna, salmon and other seafood make excellent carpaccio; just garnish with your favourite citrus. Vegetables such as zucchini—or even apple and other fruits—work well garnished with shaved cheese and toasted or candied nuts.*

Spiced Parsnip and Cauliflower Soup

Serves 4 to 6

With its elegant ivory colour and sweet, complex flavour, the parsnip *(Pastinaca sativa)* is the queen of root vegetables. It can be used in everything from soups to main courses, and when combined with some melted butter and brown sugar or honey for a side dish, it tastes just like candy. Although the parsnip has never gained great popularity here in the Prairies, it is especially well suited to our short growing season and cool climate. The parsnip is best eaten late in autumn, once it has benefited from exposure to frost. Unlike its cousin the carrot, the parsnip has no vitamin A, but it has more vitamin C.

2 to 3 Tbsp (30 to 45 mL) olive oil

1 Tbsp (15 mL) yellow mustard seeds

2 onions, finely chopped

2 garlic cloves, minced

1 tsp (5 mL) fresh ginger, finely chopped

1 Tbsp (15 mL) turmeric

1 tsp (5 mL) cardamom

1 tsp (5 mL) cumin

1 lb (500 g) cauliflower, trimmed and cut into florets

1 lb (500 g) parsnips, peeled and cut into chunks roughly the same size as the cauliflower

2 cups (500 mL) vegetable or chicken stock or water

1⅔ cups (400 mL) coconut milk

sea salt and freshly ground pepper to taste

1 Tbsp (15 mL) fresh cilantro, finely chopped

Heat olive oil in a large saucepan over medium-high heat. When oil is hot, add mustard seeds and cook until they begin to pop. Add onion, garlic and ginger, and cook for a couple of minutes until onion is soft and translucent. Add turmeric, cardamom and cumin. Add cauliflower and parsnip and cook, stirring, for a couple of minutes. Add stock or water to pan and bring it slowly to a boil. Skim off any scum that comes to top and reduce soup to a simmer. Leave it to cook gently for 30 minutes, stirring it regularly.

Soup is ready when cauliflower is cooked and tender. Stir in coconut milk. Purée soup very carefully in a blender or food processor until smooth and return it to a clean saucepan. Season soup with salt and pepper, garnish with cilantro and serve.

Tip

Parsnips are best stored in a very cold location or in the refrigerator.

For a different snack, try making parsnip chips! Peel 3 or 4 parsnips lengthwise with a sharp vegetable peeler into long paper thin strips, until you've reached the central core. Heat oil in a medium-sized saucepan to 350° F (175° C) and drop parsnip strips in small batches and fry for 1 minute until crisp and golden. Drain on paper towels, season with sea salt and serve.

Curried Pumpkin Soup

Serves 4 to 6

The Prairie provinces certainly love their pumpkins. The beginning of October annually plays host to the Great White North Pumpkin Fair and Weigh-Off in Smoky Lake, Alberta, the Great Pumpkin and Scarecrow Festival in Lumsden, Saskatchewan, and the Roland Pumpkin Fair in Roland, Manitoba. Giant pumpkin contests are often featured. In 2010, the winner of Smoky Lake's weigh-off was John Lobay and his whopping 1199.2 lb (543.9 kg) pumpkin. The town of Smoky Lake even features a 12,000-pound (5443-kilogram) concrete pumpkin. Pumpkins and other squashes are New World plants that humans have cultivated as food crops for at least 7000 years. The flesh was consumed raw or roasted, the flowers and seeds were sometimes eaten and the skins could be cut into strips, dried and made into mats. Pumpkin is a nutritious winter vegetable high in vitamin C. For people who support and buy locally produced food, look out for great pumpkins in farmers' markets in fall.

splash of olive oil

2 medium yellow onions, finely chopped

2 cloves garlic, finely chopped

1 tsp (5 mL) mustard seed

1 piece of fresh ginger, 1 in (2.5 cm) wide, peeled and finely chopped

3 lbs (1.5 kg) sugar pumpkin, peeled, seeded and cut into bite-sized chunks

vegetable or chicken stock or water, enough to cover vegetables

1 tsp (5 mL) turmeric

1$\frac{2}{3}$ cups (400 mL) coconut milk

sea salt and freshly ground pepper to taste

1 small handful of cilantro leaves, finely chopped

Heat olive oil in a medium pot over medium-high heat. When oil is hot, add onion, garlic, mustard seed and ginger and cook for about 2 minutes until onion is soft and translucent. Add pumpkin chunks to pot and cook for about 2 minutes while stirring. Add stock or water and turmeric and bring slowly to a boil. Skim off any scum that comes to top and reduce heat to a simmer. Cook gently for at least 20 minutes, stirring occasionally.

When pumpkin is tender, remove from heat and carefully purée $\frac{1}{3}$ of soup with coconut milk in a blender or food processor. Return to pot. Bring back to a simmer and season with salt and pepper. Serve hot, garnished with the cilantro sprinkled on top.

Pumpkins aren't the only vegetables that have been carved at Halloween. Beets and turnips have also been at the sharp end of a carver's knife, although these days it's hard to imagine a Halloween beet touching our hearts the same way a carved pumpkin does.

Ginger Beef

Serves 6

Did you know that the popular ginger beef with the sweet sauce and crunchy texture was invented right here on the Canadian Prairies? It's true—this "Chinese" dish is really as Canadian as it gets! As the story goes, back in the mid-'70s, Calgary's Silver Inn wanted to add a beef dish to their contemporary Chinese fare. The chef modified some traditional Chinese ingredients and methods, and *voila,* the western version of ginger beef was born. This version of Ginger Beef from Jean Paré's collection is definitely a favourite—it tastes exactly like great take-out!

½ cup (125 mL) water

½ cup (125 mL) + 1½ tsp (7 mL) cornstarch

¼ cup (60 mL) liquid honey

1½ Tbsp (25 mL) oyster sauce

½ tsp (2 mL) dried crushed chilies

1 Tbsp (15 mL) sesame oil, *divided*

2 large eggs

1 Tbsp (15 mL) soy sauce

2 cloves garlic, minced, or ½ tsp (2 mL) garlic powder

1 Tbsp (15 mL) + 1½ tsp (7 mL) finely grated peeled ginger root

1¼ lbs (560 g) sirloin steak, cut across grain into ⅛ in (3 mm) thick slices

canola oil, for deep-frying

2 green onions, cut julienne

2 medium carrots, cut julienne (see Tip)

Stir water into 1½ tsp (7 mL) cornstarch in a small bowl. Add honey, oyster sauce, chilies and 2 tsp (10 mL) sesame oil. Stir. Set aside.

Beat ½ cup (125 mL) cornstarch, eggs, soy sauce, 1 tsp (5 mL) sesame oil, garlic and ginger root with a fork in a medium bowl.

Cut beef slices into ¼ to ½ in (6 mm to 1.25 cm) shreds. Add to egg mixture. Stir until coated. Marinate at room temperature for 15 minutes.

Deep-fry beef, in several batches, in hot (375° F, 190° C) canola oil for 1 to 1½ minutes, stirring and breaking pieces apart, until golden brown. Remove beef with slotted spoon to paper towels to drain. Keep warm.

Heat 2 tsp (10 mL) canola oil in medium frying pan on medium-high until hot. Add green onion, carrot and 1 Tbsp (15 mL) ginger. Stir-fry for about 2 minutes until softened. Stir honey mixture. Stir into carrot mixture until boiling and slightly thickened. Pour over beef.

Tip

To julienne, cut into very thin strips that resemble matchsticks.

Chestnut and Beef Braise

Serves 6

It seems incredible, but there are more cattle in the Prairie provinces than there are people: in 2011, there were 9.8 million cattle compared to 6.1 million people in Alberta, Saskatchewan and Manitoba combined. This recipe calls for a tougher cut of beef such as top side or round shoulder, which uses the technique of braising—to slowly cook the meat and vegetables (including chestnuts) in liquid to moisten and tenderize the meat. The slow cooking method helps to break down the tough fibres in the meat. The delicate texture and flavour of the chestnuts complements the beef nicely in this stew—it's hearty and melt-in-the-mouth delicious!

3 lbs (1.5 kg) inside round roast

sea salt and freshly ground pepper to taste

¼ cup (60 mL) canola oil or sunflower oil

1 cup (250 mL) red wine, preferably Pinot Noir

2 cups (500 mL) beef stock

1 clove garlic, crushed with a heavy knife

2 fresh Roma tomatoes, quartered

2 cups (500 mL) baby carrots

2 cups (500 mL) pearl onions

2 cups (500 mL) small white mushrooms

1 x 10 oz (283 g) jar chestnuts, drained and roughly chopped

Preheat oven to 350° F (175° C). Season meat well with salt and pepper. Heat oil in a Dutch oven and brown meat; remove from pan. Add red wine and bring to a rapid boil on high heat until liquid is reduced and any drippings are loosened from bottom of pot. Add beef stock and stir.

Return roast to pan and add remaining ingredients. Cover and cook in the oven until tender, about 1½ hours, turning occasionally. Remove meat from pan and strain out liquid, reserving vegetables. Reduce sauce until thickened. Season to taste. Place meat on a serving dish and add reserved vegetables. Serve with sauce and roasted potatoes.

Horse chestnut trees, although not common, are robust enough to grow in the Prairie climate, but their fruit is not edible.

It's easier to peel pearl onions than it looks. First, boil them in water for a couple of minutes. Drain, then immediately pour them into a bowl of ice water. Slice the end with the root off of each, and then squeeze the onion to release it from its skin.

Macadamia-roasted Pork with Maple Syrup

Serves 8 to 10

Pork is an important agricultural sector in the Prairie provinces. Manitoba's 700 pork farmers account for around 30% of the country's total pig production, with 8 million pigs being produced in 2010. Alberta raises around 3.5 million pigs annually, with Saskatchewan responsible for 2 million. In the 1950s the Lacombe, a fast-growing, high-quality meat hog, was the first breed of livestock developed in Canada—in Lacombe, Alberta, of course. Pork is much lower in fat than it has ever been, and is a very lean protein source. Today, Canada produces about 30 million pigs per year and is the world's largest pork exporter—50% of our pork is exported to over 85 countries.

Stuffing

2 Tbsp (30 mL) olive oil

1 onion, finely chopped

4 cloves garlic, roughly chopped

¼ cup (60 mL) fresh rosemary, chopped

¼ cup (60 mL) fresh thyme, chopped

2 cups (500 mL) macadamia nuts, roughly chopped

¼ cup (60 mL) chicken stock

2 Tbsp (30 mL) dry bread crumbs

1 Tbsp (15 mL) dark brown sugar

Preheat oven to 400° F (200° C). Heat olive oil in a pan and cook onions, garlic, rosemary and thyme a few minutes. Add macadamia nuts. Stir in chicken stock, bread crumbs and brown sugar, and set stuffing aside.

Turn pork loin rib roast fat-side down. Slit lengthwise, almost but not quite all the way through, to form a long pocket, leaving a ½ in (1.25 cm) border of uncut meat at each end. Sprinkle generously with salt and pepper. Fill cavity with stuffing. Tie loin together with butcher twine at 1½ in (4 cm) intervals. Slide rosemary sprigs under twine. Brush with remaining olive oil and sprinkle generously with salt and pepper. Set, fat-side up, diagonally or curved (so it fits) on a large baking sheet or jelly roll pan.

Pork

2 x 3 lb (1.5 kg) pork loin rib roasts, patted dry, room temperature

sea salt and freshly ground pepper

butcher twine or heavy-duty kitchen string

3 to 6 sprigs of fresh rosemary

1 Tbsp olive oil

(continued on next page)

For glaze, mix maple syrup, white wine and chicken broth together. Brush glaze mixture on pork.

Roast pork in oven until a meat thermometer registers 150 to 155° F (65 to 68° C), about 2 hours, occasionally brushing with pan drippings. Let rest 15 to 20 minutes out of oven, then transfer to a carving board.

To make sauce, stir juices around pan to loosen browned bits. Pour through a strainer into a small pan, and stir in port and chicken stock. Bring to simmer and cook until lightly thickened. Slice pork roast and serve with sauce.

Glaze

½ cup (125 mL) maple syrup

¼ cup (60 mL) white wine, preferably a Riesling

¼ cup (60 mL) chicken broth

Sauce

¼ cup (60 mL) port

¼ cup (60 mL) chicken stock

Chicken and Mushroom Pot Pie

Serves 4

Poultry production is an important industry in the Prairie provinces. For example, Alberta ranks fourth in the country for poultry production, with the average Albertan eating about 66 lbs (30 kg) of chicken per year, or about a pound (½ kg) per week. Chickens (*Gallus gallus domesticus*) were first domesticated from red junglefowl in Thailand around 7000 BC. They were quick to catch on as a domestic animal because they were small, inexpensive and provided a meal, either by way of the meat or the eggs. Chicken is also one of the easiest meats to digest.

2 Tbsp (30 mL) unsalted butter

1 medium yellow onion, finely chopped

2 carrots, peeled and diced

2 celery stalks, diced

1 tsp (5 mL) garlic, minced

¼ tsp (1 mL) sea salt

¼ tsp (1 mL) freshly ground black pepper

6 oz (170 g) mushrooms, sliced

½ tsp (2 mL) fresh thyme, chopped

3 bay leaves

2 Tbsp (30 mL) dry sherry

¼ cup (60 mL) flour

2 cups (500 mL) chicken stock

1 cup (250 mL) cream (10%)

3 cups (750 mL) cooked chicken, cubed

½ cup (125 mL) peas

1 Tbsp (15 mL) parsley, chopped

(continued on next page)

Preheat oven to 375° F (190° F). Butter an 8 cup (2 L) baking dish and set aside. In a large pot, melt butter over medium-high heat and add onions, carrots and celery and cook until soft, 3 to 4 minutes. Add garlic, salt and pepper and cook, stirring, for 30 seconds. Then add mushrooms, thyme, bay leaves and cook, stirring, until mushrooms are soft and have given off their liquid, about 3 minutes. Add sherry and cook until most of liquid is evaporated. Stir in flour and cook, stirring, for 2 minutes. Stirring constantly, slowly add chicken stock and cream and cook until mixture is smooth and thickened, about 5 minutes. Add chicken, peas and parsley, stir well, and cook until chicken is heated

Look for and purchase chickens that are organic, free-range animals.

through. Remove bay leaves. Pour filling into baking dish and set aside.

For pastry, mix together flour, baking powder and salt in a bowl. Rub butter into mixture using your fingertips until mixture looks like coarse crumbs. Gently fold in buttermilk until mixture just comes together. Roll out dough on a floured surface and shape to fit top of baking dish.

Lay pastry on top of filling and score pastry slightly with a knife, so it is easier to cut after baking. Brush with egg and bake for 20 to 25 minutes or until crust is golden brown.

Pastry

2 cups (500 mL) flour

1 Tbsp (15 mL) baking powder

¼ tsp (1 mL) sea salt

6 Tbsp (90 mL) cold butter

¾ cup (175 mL) buttermilk

1 egg, beaten

Apple-roasted Pheasant

Serves 4

The ring-necked pheasant (*Phasianus colchicus*) is a popular upland game bird that was introduced into the Canadian Prairies in the early 20th century. It ranges mainly in the southern parts of Alberta, Saskatchewan and Manitoba, where it has flourished. Hunters bringing home pheasants have always been welcome in the kitchens of the Prairies, and natural populations are supplemented with hatchery birds. Pheasant is available at specialty meat markets, farmers' markets and some grocery stores. Nowadays, the Canadian Pheasant Company, located in Brooks, Alberta, is western Canada's largest pheasant producer, rearing about 200,000 pheasants every year. This recipe can also be made with other poultry, such as quail or chicken.

4 pheasant breasts, skin on, wing attached

sea salt and freshly cracked black pepper

1 Tbsp (15 mL) butter

1 Tbsp (15 mL) grape seed oil or olive oil

4 cups (1 L) Pink Lady apples, peeled and sliced

¼ cup (60 mL) honey

1 Tbsp (15 mL) garlic, minced

1 tsp (5 mL) cinnamon

1 tsp (5 mL) cloves

juice of ½ lemon

Preheat oven to 425° F (220° C). Season pheasant with salt and pepper. Heat butter and oil in an ovenproof sauté pan that is large enough to comfortably fit all meat. On medium-high heat, sear pheasant breasts, skin-side down, for 3 to 4 minutes until golden brown. Set aside.

Combine apples, honey, garlic, cinnamon, cloves and lemon in a mixing bowl and sauté in same pan as pheasant. When apples are nicely caramelized, about 5 minutes, place pheasant on top, skin-sides up, and roast in oven for 10 to 12 minutes until meat is cooked through.

Serve breasts atop a spoonful of caramelized apples.

For extra flavour, try preparing this recipe by roasting the pheasant on your barbecue. Use some apple wood chips under the grate to add some smoky apple notes to the dish.

Native to Japan and China, the pheasant is a member of the Phasianidae family of birds, which include the quail and the peacock. Terrestrial birds that can be distinguished by the male's ornate plumage, pheasants were introduced into North America in 1881.

Steamed Artichokes with Lemon Butter

Serves 4 as an appetizer

Artichokes take a bit of extra effort to grow on the Prairies, but you can find them at farmers' markets and in grocery stores across the region. Recipes calling simply for artichokes refer to the globe artichoke *(Cynara scolymus)*, which was brought to North America by French and Spanish immigrants. Artichoke is a perennial thistle first cultivated in Naples in the 15th century. According to legend, Zeus fell in love with a mortal beauty named Cynara, and, when she angered him, he threw her back to earth as the thorny artichoke. In early Greek and Roman times, artichokes were considered an aphrodisiac and, because of their reputed sexual power, were reserved for consumption only by men. Much later, in 1947, the as-yet unknown Marilyn Monroe was named "Miss California Artichoke Queen"—no doubt it was a sign of things to come.

4 smallish globe artichokes

1 clove garlic, minced, finely chopped

1 bay leaf

zest and juice from 2 lemons

¼ cup (60 mL) vegetable stock

¼ cup (60 mL) white wine

½ lb (250 g) butter

Use scissors to trim thorny tips from artichokes and trim off top, about ⅓ in (8 mm). Steam, stem-end up, in a basket over water with garlic, bay leaf and lemon zest. Cook 30 to 35 minutes or until tender. Heat vegetable stock and white wine in a medium pan and reduce to about 2 Tbsp (30 mL).

Meanwhile, cut butter into cubes. When stock has reduced, lower heat and whisk butter in 1 cube at a time until you have used all butter and sauce is thick. Stir in lemon juice to taste. Place butter sauce over low heat, being careful not to let it boil. Serve warm artichokes with butter sauce.

Tip
To prevent discolouration through oxidation, sprinkle or rub the cut surfaces of artichokes with lemon juice.

Tip
Artichokes are also available canned and frozen, and you can jazz up a homemade pizza by including them as a topping.

Cauliflower and Potato Gratin

Serves 6 to 8

You don't have to go all the way to the Netherlands to get your hands on some amazing Gouda. Amazing? Try Sylvan Star Cheese—grand champion of the Dairy Farmers of Canada's Canadian Cheese Grand Prix in 2000, finalist for best artisan farmhouse cheese in 2004, and three-category champion in 2006, including best artisan farmhouse cheese and best flavoured cheese. When John and Janny Schalkwyk immigrated to Canada, they brought with them a passion for cheese and a Dutch-sized capacity for hard work. Each day starts around 4 AM with the milking of over 85 Holstein cows. Then they get to work turning and hand-waxing 700 plus cheeses. Sylvan Star Cheese produces 12,500 pounds (25,000 kilograms) of cheese each year.

1½ cups (375 mL) Gruyere cheese, grated

½ cup (125 mL) Parmesan cheese, grated

1 medium onion, diced

1 Tbsp (15 mL) butter

2 cloves garlic, minced

2 cups (500 mL) heavy cream (32%)

1 tsp (5 mL) freshly grated nutmeg

4 lbs (2 kg) Yukon Gold potatoes, peeled and thinly sliced

2 medium cauliflower, sliced ¼ in (6 mm) thick

sea salt and freshly ground pepper

¼ cup (60 mL) fresh thyme, chopped

Butter an 8 cup (2 L) shallow baking dish and preheat oven to 350° F (175° C). Combine cheeses, reserving ½ cup (125 mL) for topping. Set aside.

Sauté onion in butter until soft. Add garlic and cook for 2 minutes. Add cream, bring just to boil and remove from heat. Stir in nutmeg. Layer potatoes and cauliflower in baking dish, seasoning each layer with salt, pepper, thyme and a sprinkle of cheeses. Continue layering until you have used all potatoes and cauliflower, and pour cream over vegetables. Top with reserved cheese. Cover and bake for 35 to 40 minutes or until vegetables are tender. Remove cover and continue cooking until top is golden brown, about 10 more minutes. Let rest at least 10 minutes or up to ½ hour before serving.

Gratins can be made with vegetables such as *zucchini, winter squash, tomatoes and leeks. They make a perfect meal together with some crusty French bread.*

Sesame Chili Vegetable Skewers

Serves 4

What can you do with all that zucchini that grows unbelievably well across the Prairies? You're not stuck making zucchini cake after zucchini cake. You can feature zucchini and other flavourful vegetables in savoury dishes like these vegetarian skewers as well. The colourful medley of veggies is accented by an Asian-inspired baste in this recipe from Company's Coming.

32 red pepper pieces, 1 in (2.5 cm) each

8 peeled jicama pieces, 1 in (2.5 cm) wide and ¼ in (6 mm) thick

8 small whole white mushrooms

8 onion pieces, 1 in (2.5 cm) thick

8 zucchini slices, ½ in (1.25 cm) thick

8 bamboo skewers (6 in [15 cm] each), soaked in water for 10 minutes

⅓ cup (75 mL) sesame oil

1 Thai hot chili pepper, minced (see Tip)

2 tsp (10 mL) finely grated ginger root

2 tsp (10 mL) sugar

½ tsp (2 mL) salt

Thread red pepper, jicama, mushrooms, onion and zucchini onto skewers.

Combine sesame oil, chili pepper, ginger root, sugar and salt. Cook skewers on a greased grill on medium for 10 to 15 minutes, brushing occasionally with sesame oil mixture, until vegetables are tender-crisp. Brush with sesame oil mixture and transfer to a serving plate.

Tip

Hot peppers contain capsaicin in the seeds and ribs, so removing them will reduce the amount of heat. When handling hot peppers, avoid touching your eyes. Be sure to wash your hands well afterwards.

If you prefer, you can use metal skewers, which of course don't need to be soaked before grilling.

The way you cut your vegetables can greatly affect presentation. Crinkle cutters can be used, and even just cutting at a different angle shows you care enough to think about how your food is displayed. But when working with skewers, make sure each vegetable piece is cut roughly the same size to ensure even cooking.

Roasted Jerusalem Artichokes

Serves 4 as a side dish

Also known as "sunchoke" and "Canada potato," the Jerusalem artichoke *(Helianthus tuberosus)* is easy to grow here and will even produce a display of small sunflowers late in the summer. In the Prairies, Jerusalem artichokes are best harvested in the fall when light frosts enhance the natural sweetness. A tuber native to North America, the Jerusalem artichoke's waxy flesh has the texture of a crispy apple and the flavour reminiscent of sunflower seeds. Traditionally, the tubers were simply boiled and eaten much like potatoes, and they can be used in place of potatoes in many recipes. The first written record of this edible member of the sunflower family dates from 1603, when Samuel de Champlain encountered it growing in the vegetable gardens of First Nations peoples.

4 cloves garlic, chopped

2½ Tbsp (37 mL) extra virgin olive oil

1½ lbs (680 g) Jerusalem artichokes

sea salt and freshly ground black pepper to taste

1 Tbsp (15 mL) chopped fresh parsley

Preheat oven to 350° F (175° C). Heat garlic and olive oil in a small pot and cook until soft. Peel Jerusalem artichokes and cut into small chunks, placing chunks into a bowl of acidulated water (see Tip) as you work. Put in a shallow roasting pan large enough to hold all in one layer comfortably. Strain garlic from oil and pour oil over chokes. Add salt and pepper and toss.

Bake in oven for about 20 minutes, stirring once or twice, until tender. Sprinkle parsley on top and serve.

 The Jerusalem artichoke has no ties to the famous Biblical city; the name simply comes from the English misunderstanding the Italian word girasol, *which means "sunflower."*

Tip

Acidulated water is just water to which a little acid normally lemon or lime juice or vinegar—has been added; ½ tsp (2 mL) per cup (250 mL) is enough. When you are peeling or cutting fruits or vegetables that discolour quickly when exposed to air, like apples, place them in acidulated water to prevent browning. Jerusalem artichokes, globe artichokes and salsify are just some of the foods that benefit from this treatment. Acidulated water is also sometimes used for cooking.

Pancetta and Pine Nut Brussels Sprouts

Serves 6

Because they does well in cool climates, Brussels sprouts (*Brassica oleracea* var. *gemmifera*) are perfectly suited to the Prairies; they even improve in flavour, sweetness and tenderness if allowed to chill through a few frosts. Brussels sprouts came originally from the region around Afghanistan and, like cauliflower, are actually a variety of cabbage. The vegetable was reputedly first cultivated in large quantities in Belgium, hence its name. Because Brussels sprouts are often overcooked, they do not tend to hold a place among the stars of the vegetable kingdom. Overcooking releases the sprouts' naturally occurring sulfur, giving them a pungent smell and taste. When properly cooked—especially if given an opportunity to "ripen" during a frost—this vegetable is sweet and nutty, and provides many nutritional benefits, such as vitamins C and D, folic acid and dietary fibre.

2 lbs (1 kg) Brussels sprouts

splash of olive oil

5 oz (140 g) pancetta, diced

sea salt and freshly ground pepper to taste

½ cup (125 mL) pine nuts, toasted (see Tip)

Preheat oven to 400° F (205° C). Slice Brussels sprouts in half lengthwise, removing any loose, outer leaves and trimming bottom stems. Toss in olive oil, add pancetta and season with salt and pepper. Spread in a single layer on a baking sheet. Stir occasionally so Brussels sprouts cook evenly.

Bake for 20 to 30 minutes until pancetta is crispy. Toss with pine nuts and another splash of olive oil, if desired.

Tip

To toast pine nuts, place in a dry frying pan and cook on low heat, stirring occasionally until lightly golden.

Pancetta is an Italian variety of bacon that has been cured with spices but not smoked like most other types of bacon. It is available at most delis and Italian markets. It is usually rolled into a sausage-like shape, and when sliced is patterned with swirls. It will keep in the fridge for up to three weeks and in the freezer for up to six months.

Maple Candied Sweet Potatoes

Serves 4 to 6

Another indigenous tuber, the sweet potato (*Ipomoea batatas*) is a traditional Prairie accompaniment to Thanksgiving dinner. Probably dating back to Peru as early as 8000 BC, the sweet potato is often confused with the yam, a vegetable distantly related to the potato. Although not commonly eaten, the leaves and shoots of the sweet potato plant are also edible and make an interesting addition to salads. Some of the best varieties of sweet potato to grow in the Prairie provinces include "Select" and "Superior," which are productive and well suited to our northern climate. "Beauregard" and "Centennial" are both ready in 90 days, making them a good choice for shorter growing seasons.

1 cup (250 mL) maple syrup

1 cup (250 mL) orange juice

½ cup (125 mL) fresh lime juice

½ cup (125 mL) water

3 lbs (1.5 kg) sweet potatoes

¼ cup (60 mL) melted butter

Combine maple syrup, fruit juices and water in a nonreactive saucepan large enough to hold all sweet potatoes comfortably. Bring to a boil, then reduce to a simmer.

Peel sweet potatoes, slicing longer ones in half, and place in saucepan. Cook, turning occasionally, for about 1½ hours or until edges of sweet potatoes turn slightly translucent and they are tender.

Transfer onto a serving platter and drizzle with butter.

Sweet potatoes are a good source of vitamin A, vitamin C and dietary fibre.

〰 Ipomoea batatas *is a vigorous, twining, climbing annual vine that is grown in containers for its attractive foliage rather than its flowers.*

Rhubarb Ginger Chutney

Makes about 5¼ cups (1.3 L)

We often use rhubarb in pies and other places we'd normally use fruits, but rhubarb is actually a vegetable that is perfectly suited for growing in the short growing season of the Canadian prairies. This tart, gingery chutney from the Company's Coming collection is a wonderful reason to get the canner out. It uses up a goodly amount of fresh rhubarb from your (or your neighbour's) backyard patch. Enjoy it alongside roast pork for a change from applesauce.

2 tsp (10 mL) canola oil

1½ cups (375 mL) chopped onion

6 cups (1.5 L) chopped fresh (or frozen) rhubarb

1 cup (250 mL) apple cider vinegar

1 cup (250 mL) brown sugar, packed

1 cup (250 mL) dark raisins

⅓ cup (75 mL) finely chopped ginger root

2 tsp (10 mL) dry mustard

½ tsp (2 mL) ground cinnamon

½ tsp (2 mL) ground coriander

¼ tsp (1 mL) ground allspice

¼ tsp (1 mL) salt

¼ tsp (1 mL) pepper

⅓ cup (75 mL) minced crystallized ginger

Heat canola oil in Dutch oven on medium. Add onion. Cook for about 10 minutes, stirring often, until softened.

Add rhubarb, vinegar, brown sugar, raisins, ginger root, dry mustard, cinnamon, coriander, allspice, salt and pepper. Stir. Bring to a boil on medium. Boil gently, uncovered, for about 20 minutes until rhubarb is tender.

Add crystallized ginger. Stir well. Fill 5 hot sterile 1 cup (250 mL) jars to within ½ in (1.25 cm) of top. Remove air bubbles and adjust headspace if necessary. Wipe rims. Place hot metal lids on jars and screw on metal bands fingertip tight. Do not over-tighten. Process in boiling water bath for 15 minutes (see Tip). Remove jars. Let stand at room temperature until cool. Store in refrigerator for up to 1 month after opening.

Tip

Processing time is for elevations 1001 to 3000 feet (306 to 915 m) above sea level. Adjust the processing time for elevation in your area if necessary.

Canning used to be an essential practice for people on the Canadian Prairies—a way to preserve food for the long, cold winter ahead. Today, canning is a great way to use up surpluses of fruits or vegetables, and makes for a fantastic, thoughtful homemade gift.

Creamy Espresso Martini

Serves 1

Two-thirds of adults on the Prairies drink coffee every day, and its caffeine content and flavour have made coffee the second most popular beverage choice after water. Coffee (*Coffea* species) was discovered in Ethiopia—legend has it by a farmer who noticed his goat's boisterous behaviour after eating some berries. Only when the berries (they are actually seeds, not beans) reached Turkey in the 15th century were they roasted and crushed to make an early version of today's beverage. The coffee industry today employs an astounding 20 million people and is second in value only to petroleum products in international trade.

1 oz (30 mL) cold espresso

1½ oz (45 mL) coffee- or vanilla-flavoured vodka

1½ oz (45 mL) coffee liqueur

1 oz (30 mL) Irish cream liqueur

1 scoop (¼ cup [60 mL]) vanilla ice cream

Pour all ingredients into a cocktail shaker and shake vigorously, and strain into a chilled martini glass.

The Prairie Coffee Project, a group of cafés and coffee roasters from Alberta, Saskatchewan and Manitoba, hosts an annual competition for baristas from across the Prairie provinces.

 *Did you know that most people employed to grow and harvest coffee beans live well below the poverty line and receive little income for their labour? To help you enjoy your java guilt-free, we recommend you seek out and purchase Fair Trade organically grown coffee.*

Caramel-dipped Apples

Serves 8

In the Prairies, you can pick fresh apples every year at U-pick farms. For example, Sprout Farms in Bon Accord, Alberta, an apple orchard and U-pick destination, boasts over 25 years of fruit-growing experience. In the 1920s, hardy apples were first being promoted on the Prairies as a tree fruit option, but it wasn't until the 1970s that tasty and very hardy varieties such as the Norland became popular here. Many of these hardy apples were developed at the Agriculture Canada Research Centre in Morden, Manitoba. Today, apples have the honour of being Canada's number one fruit crop, with over 454,000 tons (412,000 tonnes) grown every year.

1 lb (500 g) dark brown sugar

¾ cup (175 mL) unsalted butter, room temperature

1 x 10 oz (300 mL) can sweetened condensed milk

⅔ cup (150 mL) light corn syrup

¼ tsp (1 mL) sea salt

1 tsp (5 mL) vanilla

¼ cup (60 mL) whipping cream

8 firm apples, such as Granny Smith, stems removed, washed and dried

8 wooden sticks, such as craft sticks or even chopsticks

Combine brown sugar, butter, condensed milk, corn syrup and salt in a heavy-bottomed pot over medium-low heat and stir slowly but continually to dissolve sugar until it reaches a temperature between 234 and 240° F (112 and 115° C) on a candy thermometer, or until it reaches the soft-ball stage (see Tip). Remove from heat and stir in vanilla and whipping cream. Pour into a clean metal bowl. Cool until caramel is 200° F (95° C), about 15 minutes.

While caramel is cooling, line a baking sheet with buttered parchment paper and push one stick into stem end of each apple. Dip apples in caramel and let excess caramel drip off before setting on greased paper. Cool before eating and chill any uneaten apples, wrapped in cellophane, up to one week.

Tip

The soft-ball stage is a candy test where you drop a little syrup in cold water. At the soft-ball stage, the syrup forms a soft ball that flattens when it is removed from the water.

Tip

Once the caramel apples have set, dip them into melted chocolate for an extra decadent Halloween treat. You can also roll them in chopped nuts, candy sprinkles or crushed candy bars!

Tip

If your apples are quite waxy, dip them in boiling water for 30 seconds to remove the wax. Dry very well.

Grilled Chicken and Squash

Serves 4

The many varieties of squash are divided into two broad categories: summer and winter. The winter varieties, such as butternut squash, are available year-round, but are tastiest from early fall through winter. Winter squash, with its thicker skin, is heartier and has firmer flesh—perfect for grilling. In general, winter squash also has more iron, riboflavin and Vitamin A than summer varieties. It's never too late in the year to take advantage of the natural sweetness elicited from grilled butternut squash in this attractive salad from the Company's Coming kitchen.

$1\frac{1}{4}$ lbs (560 g) boneless, skinless chicken thighs (about 6)

1 lb (500 g) butternut squash, cut into $\frac{1}{2}$ in (1.25 cm) slices

$\frac{1}{4}$ cup (60 mL) canola oil, *divided*

1 Tbsp (15 mL) sugar

1 Tbsp (15 mL) ground cinnamon

1 tsp (5 mL) salt

$\frac{1}{4}$ tsp (1 mL) pepper

8 cups (2 L) baby spinach leaves, lightly packed

$\frac{1}{2}$ cup (125 mL) coarsely chopped walnuts, toasted (see Tip)

$\frac{1}{2}$ cup (125 mL) thinly sliced red onion

2 oz (57 g) goat (chèvre) cheese, cut up

$\frac{2}{3}$ cup (150 mL) orange juice

2 Tbsp (30 mL) Dijon mustard (with whole seeds)

1 Tbsp (15 mL) brown sugar, packed

Brush chicken and squash with 2 Tbsp (30 mL) canola oil.

Combine sugar, cinnamon, salt and pepper and sprinkle over top. Grill on direct medium heat for about 5 minutes per side until chicken is no longer pink inside and squash is tender. Let stand until cool enough to handle. Slice chicken into thin strips and cut squash into cubes. Transfer to a large bowl.

Add spinach, walnuts, red onion and goat cheese and toss.

Whisk orange juice, 2 Tbsp (30 mL) canola oil, mustard and brown sugar together until sugar is dissolved. Drizzle over salad and toss.

Crusty bread makes a hearty accompaniment for any winter salad.

Tip

Toasting nuts brings out an aroma and depth of flavour not apparent in the raw product. To toast nuts, seeds or coconut, put them into an ungreased frying pan. Heat on medium for 3 to 5 minutes, stirring often, until golden. To bake, spread them evenly in an ungreased shallow pan. Bake in 350° F (175° C) oven for 5 to 10 minutes, stirring or shaking often, until golden.

Mixed Citrus Salad with Lemongrass Vinaigrette

Serves 4

Oranges, lemons and limes originated as wild fruit in Southeast Asia thousands of years ago. Their taste, colour and fragrance made them very popular, and many cultures contributed to their spread across the globe. Today, citrus fruits are cultivated in about 140 countries, with about half of the total production dedicated to oranges. Citrus fruits are particularly popular and much appreciated in winter because of their long storage qualities and refreshingly bright taste. And we can't forget the long-anticipated Christmas oranges (mandarins, clementines, satsumas), with their easy-to-peel skin and super sweet taste. They have surely become as much a part of a Christmas on the Prairies as snow and St. Nick.

2 large grapefruit, peeled and segmented

2 oranges, peeled and segmented

2 blood oranges, peeled and segmented

½ cup (125 mL) kumquat, sliced in thin rounds

1 star fruit, sliced crosswise

handful of fresh mint, chopped

Dressing

1 stalk lemongrass, tender bottom only

½ cup (125 mL) apple juice

2 Tbsp (30 mL) honey or agave syrup

1 Tbsp (15 mL) shallots, finely chopped

zest and juice from 1 lime

2 Tbsp (30 mL) canola oil or sunflower oil

Combine grapefruit, oranges, blood oranges, kumquat and star fruit in a medium-sized bowl and let sit for 15 minutes.

For the dressing, bruise and roughly chop lemongrass. In a small saucepan, combine apple juice, honey or agave juice and lemongrass. Bring to a boil and cook for 5 minutes. Remove saucepan from heat and let cool to room temperature. Add shallots, lime zest and juice and oil, and whisk together until well blended. Toss citrus fruit and mint with dressing and serve.

Oranges were not named for their colour—the word orange comes from the Sanskrit naranga, which means "fragrant." Scurvy, a condition resulting from vitamin C deficiency, was a major problem throughout the exploration and settlement of Canada. It can be prevented or cured by eating citrus fruit such as oranges.

Potato and Roasted Garlic Chowder

Serves 4

You can roast as much or as little garlic at a time as you want, and keep the leftovers for later in the week. Preheat the oven to 350° F (175° C). Slice the top of each bulb of garlic to expose the cloves, then lay them cut-side up in a baking dish. Drizzle them with olive oil and sprinkle them with sea salt. Roast for 20 to 30 minutes or until the cloves are tender. Remove the garlic from the oven and set aside until cool enough to handle. The buttery flesh of the cloves will come out of the bulb easily when you squeeze it (throw out the papery skin of the bulb). Alternatively, you can serve the whole roasted bulbs as a garnish to grilled meats or vegetables.

2 medium onions, diced

¼ cup (60 mL) unsalted butter

1 Tbsp (15 mL) olive oil

2 cups (500 mL) celery, diced

1 cup (250 mL) carrots, diced

4 medium potatoes, peeled and diced

1 bay leaf

vegetable or chicken stock, enough to just cover vegetables

2 bulbs roasted garlic (see above), cloves squeezed out and roughly chopped

2 cups (500 mL) heavy cream (32%)

sea salt and freshly ground pepper to taste

¼ cup (60 mL) fresh herbs such as parsley, thyme or mint, chopped

In a heavy pot, sauté onions in butter and olive oil until they turn golden. Add vegetables and bay leaf and cover with stock. Simmer for 15 minutes, then add roasted garlic and cream. Simmer for 10 to 15 minutes more or until potatoes are cooked and soup is reduced and creamy. Remove bay leaf. Season to taste with salt and pepper. Ladle soup into bowls and garnish with a sprinkle of herbs.

The first potatoes to grow in the Prairies were from seed potatoes the early settlers brought from their homelands in the 1880s.

Garlic has long been reputed to prevent everything from the common cold and flu to the plague. Even the father of antibiotic medicine, Louis Pasteur, studied the pungent plant. Pasteur noticed that some bacteria were killed when they came in contact with the "stinking rose." Although nowhere near as potent as medical antibiotics (and not to be substituted for them!), garlic supplements are taken by many people for their purported health benefits.

Warthog Ale and Cheddar Soup

Serves 4

There are a number of fine microbreweries throughout the Prairie provinces. Winnipeg boasts the Half Pints Brewing Co., and Saskatchewan's Bushwakker Brewing Co. was awarded Gold for their Tartan Tsar Russian Imperial Stout at the 2011 Canadian Brewing Awards. Ed McNally founded Alberta's most recognizable microbrewery, Big Rock Brewery, named after the huge glacial erratic in a field southwest of Okotoks. After a successful career as a lawyer, Ed began farming barley and quickly became interested in brewing beer, a childhood dream for the Lethbridge-born entrepreneur. Big Rock Brewery came to be in 1984, but it wasn't until the summer of 1986—and a strike at the big corporate breweries—that Big Rock really sank its teeth into the market. All of a sudden, the brewery had to schedule its dedicated employees in shifts around the clock to keep up with the demand for what was the only beer available during that hot summer.

2 medium onions, diced

¼ cup (60 mL) unsalted butter

1 Tbsp (15 mL) olive oil

2 cups (500 mL) celery, diced

1 cup (250 mL) parsnips, diced

4 medium potatoes, peeled and diced

1 bay leaf

vegetable or chicken stock, enough to just cover vegetables

2 cups (500 mL) heavy cream (32%)

2 cups (500 mL) sharp white Cheddar cheese, grated

½ to 1 bottle of Warthog Ale (or your choice of brown ale), about 6 to 12 oz (170 to 341 mL) or to taste

sea salt and freshly ground pepper

In a heavy pot, sauté onions in butter and oil until they turn golden. Add celery, parsnips, potatoes, bay leaf and add enough stock to cover everything. Simmer for 15 minutes, then add cream and simmer for 10 to 15 minutes more or until potatoes are cooked and soup is reduced and creamy. Remove soup from heat and blend in cheese in small batches. Return to medium-low heat and stir in ale to taste. Season with salt and pepper and serve.

Canadians spend over $6.7 billion per year on beer, accounting for more than 51% of the sales of all alcohol in the country combined.

The Okotoks erratic is a huge chunk of rock weighing 16,500 tons (16,700 tonnes) brought from Jasper National Park to its current destination by the flow of glacial ice 10,000 years ago. The Big Rock, which figures in Blackfoot stories, is a famous landmark that is impossible to overlook.

Hearty Saskatchewan Lentil Soup

Serves 4 to 6

Lentils are pulses or legumes, a group of plants where the seed is grown in a pod; for example, chickpeas and beans. Very high in protein and essential amino acids and endowed with a long storage life, lentils are an important crop worldwide. Canada is the world's largest exporter of lentils, with the majority of lentils imported by India. Saskatchewan produces the bulk of Canada's lentils, and its lentils are exported to over 130 countries. Over 6 million acres (2.5 million hectares) of land is dedicated to lentil production is Saskatchewan every year. Lentils should be a staple in every pantry; they cook quickly, are delicious in salads and soups and can be used as a meat substitute in many dishes, such as meat loaf and burgers.

½ tsp (2 mL) cinnamon

¼ tsp (1 mL) cloves

1 Tbsp (15 mL) cumin

2 tsp (10 mL) olive oil

1 cup (250 mL) onions, chopped

1 clove garlic, minced

½ cup (125 mL) carrot, diced

1 large bay leaf

½ in (1.25 cm) piece of fresh ginger, peeled and chopped

2 cups (500 mL) dried red lentils, rinsed

water

1 Tbsp (15 mL) apple cider vinegar

2 tsp (10 mL) cilantro, chopped

salt and freshly ground pepper to taste

finely sliced chives for garnish

In a small pan, toast cinnamon, cloves and cumin until very fragrant, about 1 to 2 minutes. Set aside.

In a medium-sized pot, heat olive oil over medium-high heat and sauté onions until translucent. Add garlic, carrot, bay leaf, ginger and toasted cinnamon, cloves and cumin and sauté about 2 minutes. Add lentils and add enough water to cover by 1 in (2.5 cm) and cook 30 to 45 minutes or until lentils are completely soft. Stir in apple cider vinegar and cilantro. Remove bay leaf. Season with salt and plenty of pepper. Garnish each serving with chives.

A product of the Prairies is the best way to describe Joe St. Denis's peabutter. No, that's not a typo. A veteran pea farmer of 20 years on his Legal farm north of Edmonton, St. Denis came up with the idea to produce an allergy-free alternative to peanut butter. Peanuts are Canada's number one allergy-producing food, creating reactions that are often so severe that many schools have banned its inclusion in children's lunch boxes. Thanks to St. Denis and his "NoNuts Peabutter," which not only looks but also tastes like the real thing, everyone can enjoy peabutter and jelly sandwiches without fear.

Tomato and Feta-stuffed Sirloin

Serves 6

Feta cheese is a crumbly cheese with a tangy and salty flavour, often made from goat's milk. It is aged and stored in a brine solution, but if you'd like to make your feta less salty, mix the brine with an equal amount of water and let the cheese sit for two days. Oak Island Acres Goat Dairy in Ile des Chenes, Manitoba, produces dairy products such as goat's milk and feta cheese. At their family-run farm, they take care of 250 to 400 goats.

½ cup (125 mL) sun-dried tomatoes in oil

4 cloves garlic, crushed

⅓ cup (75 mL) olive oil, *divided*

2 to 3 lbs (1 to 1.5 kg) beef sirloin tip roast

1 cup (250 mL) feta cheese, crumbled

3 Tbsp (45 mL) chopped fresh oregano

⅓ cup (75 mL) lemon juice

salt and pepper

Combine sun-dried tomatoes, garlic and 2 Tbsp (30 mL) olive oil in a blender or food processor until smooth.

Place roast, fat-side up, on a cutting board. Using a sharp knife, cut horizontally lengthwise about ½ in (1.25 cm) from bottom, almost but not quite through to other side. Open flat. Cut horizontally through thicker half of roast about ½ in (1.25 cm), almost but not quite through to other side. Open flat.

Spread tomato–oil mixture over roast, leaving ½ in (1.25 cm) border. Crumble feta over top. Sprinkle with oregano. Roll up tightly, jelly-roll style, starting from short edge. Tie with butcher's string at 1 in (2.5 cm) intervals.

Place roast in a large dish and drizzle with lemon juice and remaining olive oil, turning roast to ensure it is well coated. Cover and let stand in refrigerator for about 1 hour, turning every 20 minutes. Place roast in frying pan on medium and cook, rotating, for about 3 minutes per side until all sides are seared. Place roast on a greased rack in a roaster and cook in a 375° F (190° C) oven for about 1¼ hours until internal temperature of roast reaches 145° F (63° C) for medium-rare or until roast reaches desired doneness.

For a hearty winter meal, serve with roasted potatoes tossed with a bit of olive oil and your choice of spices, and some colourful vegetables.

Feta is often made with goat's milk, but some people prefer the feta that is made with sheep's milk. Sheep's milk feta tends to be a bit milder. Traditional feta cheese from Greek is made with sheep's milk, or sheep's milk mixed with up to 30% with goat milk.

Cabbage Rolls

Makes 60

Cooks love to make little packages of food for their families, and cabbage leaves lend themselves particularly well to this task. Because cabbage rolls appear in so many cuisines, spanning continents, languages and centuries, it is difficult to pin down their origin. Large numbers of Ukrainian settlers came to settle in what is now the parkland of the Canadian Prairies beginning in the early 1890s, bringing their version of stuffed cabbage rolls, Borscht and pierogi. Many of us have fond memories of a kitchen full of women—from multiple generations of family—making dozens and dozens of delicious cabbage rolls for an upcoming holiday meal or feast at a special gathering. Although cabbage rolls can be a tad time-consuming, the effort is always appreciated.

1 large head of green cabbage (about 5 lbs [2.3 kg])

boiling water, to cover

2$\frac{1}{4}$ cups (550 mL) + $\frac{2}{3}$ cup (150 mL) water

1$\frac{1}{2}$ cups (375 mL) short grain white rice

1$\frac{1}{2}$ tsp (7 mL) salt

$\frac{1}{2}$ tsp (2 mL) pepper

6 bacon slices, diced

2 cups (500 mL) finely chopped onion

1 cup (250 mL) tomato juice

1 Tbsp (15 mL) butter (or hard margarine)

Remove core from cabbage. Trim about $\frac{1}{2}$ in (1.25 cm) slice from bottom. Place, cut-side down, in a Dutch oven or large pot. Cover with boiling water. Cover Dutch oven with foil. Heat on medium-low for about 30 minutes, using tongs to remove leaves to tea towel as they start to soften and loosen. Blot dry. Cut 'V' shape along tough ribs of leaves to remove. Discard ribs. Cut larger leaves into 2 equal pieces. Set aside.

Measure 2$\frac{1}{4}$ cups (550 mL) water into a medium saucepan. Bring to a boil. Add rice, salt and pepper. Stir. Reduce heat to medium-low. Simmer, covered, for about 10 minutes, without stirring, until liquid is absorbed but rice is still firm. Transfer to a large bowl. Fluff with a fork. Cool.

Cook bacon in a large frying pan on medium for about 10 minutes until starting to brown. Add onion. Cook for about 10 minutes, stirring often, until onion is very soft. Add to rice. Mix well. Spoon about 1$\frac{1}{2}$ Tbsp (25 mL) rice mixture onto centre of 1 cabbage leaf. Fold sides over filling. Roll up tightly from bottom to enclose. Repeat with remaining cabbage leaves and rice mixture. Arrange cabbage rolls tightly together, seam-side down, in layers in a greased large roasting pan. Layer any remaining cabbage leaves on top of rolls.

Combine tomato juice, $\frac{2}{3}$ cup (150 mL) water and butter in small saucepan. Heat and stir on medium until hot. Pour over cabbage rolls. Bake, covered, in a 350° F (175° C) oven for about 1$\frac{1}{2}$ hours until liquid is absorbed and cabbage rolls are tender.

Tip

Cabbage rolls, also known as *holubtsi* by our Ukrainian friends, can be quite delicate. To avoid sticking and tearing, make sure your cooking vessel is well greased. And if you want to make cleanup a snap, you can line your cooking vessel with well-greased foil or parchment paper.

Other small packets of food from various cuisines now popular in the Prairies include dolmades and spanakopita (Greek), samosas (Indian), calzones (Italian), cornish pasties (Scottish), spring rolls and wontons (Asian).

Mundare Sausage Stew

Serves 6

Synonymous with winter and cold, a stew is simply thick soup with chunky cuts of vegetables, meat or seafood—or a combination thereof. Offering a hearty and frugal meal that keeps for many days, stews freeze well and can be made in large quantities to feed many, all in the convenience of one pot. In the Prairies, many popular stews such as goulash, gumbo and Irish stew enjoy long culinary histories. The stew given here is made from homegrown ingredients: the village of Mundare is home of the famous Stawnichy's kielbassa, a Ukrainian-style sausage for which the town is best known. The business has won numerous awards for its superior products since it was founded in 1959 with only one smokehouse.

1 to 2 Tbsp (15 to 30 mL) canola oil

$\frac{3}{4}$ lb (340 g) Mundare sausage, cut into $\frac{1}{4}$ in (6 mm) slices

1 yellow onion, diced

2 medium carrots, peeled and sliced diagonally

2 celery stalks, sliced diagonally

$\frac{1}{2}$ cup (125 mL) dry white wine

6 cloves garlic, finely chopped

$\frac{3}{4}$ lb (340 g) venison, cut into 1 in (2.5 cm) pieces (see Tip)

1 x 19 oz (540 mL) can crushed tomatoes

4 cups (1 L) vegetable stock

2 Tbsp (30 mL) fresh thyme or 1 tsp (5 mL) dried thyme

$\frac{1}{4}$ cup (60 mL) fresh parsley, chopped

1 tsp (5 mL) salt

pinch of chipotle powder or cayenne

freshly ground pepper

In a large pot, heat canola oil over moderately high heat. Add Mundare sausage and cook, stirring frequently, until lightly browned and heated through, about 5 minutes.

Add onion and cook, stirring occasionally, about 5 minutes, then add carrots and celery and cook for another 5 minutes. Add white wine and garlic, bring to a simmer, and cook until reduced to about $\frac{1}{4}$ cup (60 mL), about 3 minutes. Add venison, tomatoes, vegetable stock, thyme, parsley, salt and chipotle powder. Cover, bring to a simmer and cook for 20 minutes. Add freshly ground pepper, and taste and adjust seasoning, if necessary.

Tip

Bison can be used in place of the venison.

To recognize the contribution to the community by the Stawnichys, a 42-foot (12.8-metre) high, 6-ton statue of their famous kielbassa was erected in 2001, and it has become a popular Alberta roadside attraction.

Honey and Herb Brined Turkey

Serves 14 to 16

More and more people are turning to brining to ensure a moist and flavourful turkey, and it really is the best way. If you haven't tried it yet, now's the time. You'll get the best results from brining for 18 hours, but you'll notice benefits from as little as a two-hour dip in the brine. But we don't recommend stuffing your brined turkey, because you're likely to end up with stuffing that is too salty. Cook it separately instead.

8 qts (8 L) warm water

2 cups (500 mL) coarse salt

1 cup (250 mL) honey

⅓ cup (75 mL) lightly packed sprigs of fresh rosemary

⅓ cup (75 mL) lightly packed fresh thyme sprigs

⅓ cup (75 mL) fresh sage leaves

8 cloves of garlic

2 Tbsp (30 mL) cracked black pepper

1 x 18 to 20 lb (8 to 9 kg) turkey

½ cup (125 mL) butter

salt and freshly ground pepper

(continued on next page)

For brine, combine water and salt in large stockpot. Stir until salt has dissolved. Add honey and stir until combined. Stir in rosemary, thyme, sage, garlic and pepper. Add turkey. Place a large, heavy plate on top of turkey to submerge it completely in brine. Refrigerate for 12 to 18 hours.

Preheat oven to 450° F. Drain turkey well and discard brine. Pat turkey dry inside and out. Tuck wings under turkey and tie legs together loosely. Transfer to rack in roasting pan. Rub turkey with butter and sprinkle generously with salt and pepper. Place roasting pan in oven. Reduce oven temperature to 325° F. Roast until thermometer inserted into thickest part of thigh registers 175° F (80° C), about 2½ hours. Transfer to serving platter and tent with foil. Let turkey rest at least 30 minutes before carving (internal temperature will rise 5 to 10 degrees while standing, bringing your bird up to or past the 180° F [82° C] mark for fully cooked poultry).

Tip

Roasted turkey is a tried-and-true traditional dish for the holiday season. Try it with side dishes like Pancetta and Pine Nut Brussels Sprouts (p. 108), Maple Candied Sweet Potatoes (p. 110), Cauliflower and Potato Gratin (p. 102) or Balsamic-glazed Root Vegetables (p. 144).

While turkey is resting, make gravy. Spoon off fat from pan drippings, reserving ¼ cup (60 mL) fat. Measure out ⅔ cup (150 mL) pan juices. In large saucepan over medium heat, melt butter and reserved ¼ cup (60 mL) fat. Stir in flour. Cook, stirring constantly, until light brown, about 2 minutes. Whisk in broth, pear juice and reserved ⅔ cup (150 mL) pan juices. Simmer, stirring, until thickened, about 10 minutes. Stir in rum. Season to taste with salt and pepper.

Tip

If you don't have a stockpot big enough to fit your turkey, line a cooler with a large, clean, heavy-duty plastic garbage bag. Place turkey and brine inside bag. Cover turkey with plate to submerge, then tie up the bag and close the cooler lid. Place cooler in refrigerator.

If the stockpot doesn't fit in your refrigerator, use the cooler option above, and keep it in a cool place (about 39° F [4° C]), such as a garage. If you think the cool place might not be cold enough, monitor the temperature every few hours and add freezer packs to your cooler as necessary.

Pear Gravy

¼ cup (60 mL) butter

½ cup (125 mL) all-purpose flour

2 cups (500 mL) low-sodium chicken broth

1 cup (250 mL) pear juice

2 Tbsp (30 mL) dark rum

salt and freshly ground pepper

Citrus Perch

Serves 4

Perch (*Perca flavescens*) are found in lakes and rivers throughout the Prairies, and they are one of our top sport fishes. The first recorded sighting of this native fish in Alberta was in 1919, in both Pine Lake and Sylvan Lake. And in Manitoba, Duck Mountain Provincial Park's East Blue Lake offers some fantastic perch fishing (and many other varieties of sport fish). Adult perch weigh in at around a pound (half a kilogram), and they are most popular during ice-fishing season because, unlike many other fish, they feed year-round. The Prairies offer a multitude of fishing guides who know exactly where to go for your next search for this popular fish.

1 lemon

1 lime

1 orange

3 to 4 lb (1.5 to 2 kg) fresh lake perch, gutted and filleted

2 Tbsp (30 mL) butter

sea salt and freshly ground pepper

Preheat grill to 450° F (230° C). Thinly slice lemon, lime and orange. Layer fish, fruit and butter on aluminum foil, seasoning each layer with salt and pepper. Wrap foil around fish, making sure it is well sealed, and cook on grill for 7 to 10 minutes.

Tip

This versatile recipe can also be used to cook fresh fish over the campfire. Try it with your favourite catch-of-the-day.

Tip

If you're purchasing fish, you want to make sure that it's fresh. Check that:

- the flesh colour is bright and consistent
- the fish smells fresh and not "fishy"
- the flesh is firm, elastic and moist—but not slimy
- the cut edges are neat and clean.

Eggplant Lasagna

Serves 6 to 8

Eggplant (*Solanum melongena*), like its cousin the tomato, was long believed to be poisonous (well, more accurately, thought to drive people mad) and got off to a slow start in gardens outside of the Mediterranean, except as an ornamental plant. Eggplant is unique in the nightshade family as the only member to have originated in the Eastern Hemisphere—in India and China specifically. Like tomatoes, peppers and potatoes, eggplants come in a wide variety of shapes and colours, although globe-shaped varieties such as "Black Beauty" are most common in grocery stores here. Eggplants need a lot of sun and heat to grow, so most Prairie farms grow their eggplants in hothouses to secure a reliable supply. By the way, eggplant got its name because early varieties introduced to Europe were white and looked like eggs!

1 large eggplant, sliced ½ in (1.25 cm) thick, crosswise

1 medium zucchini, sliced ½ in (1.25 cm) thick

2 to 3 Tbsp (30 to 45 mL) olive oil

sea salt and freshly ground pepper

Tomato Sauce

2 Tbsp (30 mL) butter

1 Tbsp (15 mL) olive oil

2 large onions, finely chopped

3 or 4 cloves garlic, minced

2 bay leaves

sea salt and freshly ground pepper to taste

splash of red wine

2 cups (500 mL) canned plum tomatoes, roughly chopped, juice reserved

Toss eggplant and zucchini slices with olive oil and season with salt and pepper. Grill on a stovetop grill or barbecue for 5 minutes on each side. Set aside.

Preheat oven to 375° F (190° C). Warm butter and olive oil in a heavy-based casserole over medium heat. Add onion and sauté for about 5 minutes until softened and translucent. Add garlic and cook for another couple of minutes, stirring to coat well. Cook gently for about 5 minutes. Add bay leaves, salt and pepper. Pour in wine and simmer until it has evaporated, then add tomatoes with their juice and stir thoroughly. Cook, uncovered, for 30 minutes. Taste and correct seasoning.

For ricotta mixture, combine ingredients in medium bowl. Season to taste and set aside.

For béchamel, pour milk into a saucepan with bay leaves, onion and a generous pinch of nutmeg. Bring to just below boiling point, then remove from heat and leave to infuse for 10 minutes. Strain milk to remove bay leaves and onion.

Tip

You can add as many layers as you wish, depending on the size of your pan.

(continued on next page)

Melt butter in a saucepan and stir in flour. Cook, stirring, for 5 minutes. Pour hot milk into flour mixture. Cook on low heat, stirring frequently, for 10 minutes until thickened. Season sauce with salt and pepper and set aside.

To assemble, start by buttering a 13 x 9 x 3 in (33 x 23 x 7.5 cm) baking pan. Pour some béchamel into baking pan—enough to just cover bottom. Top with a layer of lasagna, add béchamel, a layer of grilled vegetables, tomato sauce, then more béchamel and a good handful of Asiago cheese. Cover with lasagna, then ricotta mixture. Top with lasagna, then béchamel, vegetables and tomato sauce. Add another layer of lasagna and top with béchamel. Add a final sprinkling of Asiago cheese. Bake for 30 to 40 minutes until browned and bubbling all over.

Tip

Older eggplants will have an acrid flavour, so choose freshly picked eggplants, if possible. Alternatively, you can remove most of the bitter flavour by salting the sliced eggplant and letting it sit for 10 to 15 minutes. Gently squeeze out the bitter liquid, rinse lightly in cold water and pat dry on paper towel.

Ricotta Mixture

2 cups (500 g) ricotta cheese

½ cup (125 mL) freshly grated Parmesan cheese

½ cup (125 mL) freshly grated mozzarella cheese

sea salt and freshly ground pepper

Béchamel

3 cups (750 mL) milk

2 bay leaves

1 onion, halved

pinch of freshly grated nutmeg

¼ cup (60 mL) butter

¼ cup (60 mL) flour

sea salt and freshly ground pepper

12 sheets oven-ready lasagna noodles

2 cups (500 mL) freshly grated Asiago cheese

Caramelized Onion and Goat Cheese Tart

Serves 6

Because they are such great keepers, onions *(Allium cepa)* are a perfect winter food. They are also extremely versatile and lend themselves to many uses. They can be eaten raw or cooked, chopped or whole. Onions have been a prized food for thousands of years—they were often presented as gifts or even used as payment for goods or lodging. A naturally occurring antioxidant, quercetin, contributes to the reputation onions have for being healthy. Onions grow well in our climate, and the Prairies are home to the wild white onion *(A. textile),* known for its combined garlic and onion flavour.

1 Tbsp (15 mL) canola oil

1 Tbsp (15 mL) butter

6 medium yellow onions, thinly sliced

sea salt to taste

1 tsp (5 mL) sugar

1 Tbsp (15 mL) balsamic vinegar

Béchamel

2 Tbsp (30 mL) butter

2 Tbsp (30 mL) flour

1 cup (250 mL) milk

1 bay leaf

pinch of nutmeg

1 x ¾ lb (397 g) package frozen puff pastry, thawed

egg wash made with 1 beaten egg and a splash of water

8 oz (250 g) goat cheese

2 Tbsp (30 mL) chopped fresh herbs, such as parsley, thyme or sage (optional)

Heat canola oil and butter in a large pan over medium heat. Add onions, season with salt and cook until softened, about 6 minutes. Stir in sugar and balsamic vinegar, turn heat to medium low and cook for 30 to 45 minutes, stirring often, until nicely caramelized.

To make béchamel, melt butter in a small, heavy saucepan over low heat. Add flour and stir over low heat for 5 to 7 minutes. Slowly add milk, bay leaf and nutmeg, stirring constantly, and cook for about 10 more minutes until smooth and thick.

Preheat oven to 400° F (200° C). Roll out pastry to ⅛ in (3 mm) thick and place on a rectangular baking sheet. Prick all over with a fork. Brush outside edges, about ½ in (1.25 cm), with egg wash.

Combine onions and béchamel sauce in a bowl. Crumble in goat cheese and fresh herbs, if desired, and stir to combine. Spread onion mixture onto pastry and bake for 15 to 20 minutes until pastry is puffed and golden. Let sit 10 minutes before cutting into squares.

(continued on next page)

To make port sauce, combine port and stock in a small saucepan and reduce over medium heat until thick and syrupy.

Serve squares warm or at room temperature with a lightly dressed green salad and port sauce.

Tip

This tart is perfect for picnics, potlucks and lazy Sunday brunches. Best served at room temperature or slightly warm, it makes a great "do ahead" choice for travelling or entertaining. It also could be done in individual tart shells for easy serving.

Port Sauce

1 cup (250 mL) port

½ cup (125 mL) chicken stock

Tempura

Makes about 2¼ cups (550 mL) tempura batter

Although indulging in fried food is always tempting, it seems especially so in our cold, long winters. And if you are going to break your diet, better to do it at home where at least you can use fresh, good quality oil and ingredients. Batter-laced deep-frying is a method of cooking that was introduced to Japan by Portuguese missionaries during the 16th century. By the 17th century, Tokyo street vendors were selling *tempura*, using fish freshly caught in Tokyo Bay and most often fried in sesame oil. The word tempura comes from the Latin *ad tempora cuaresmae*, meaning "in the time of Lent"—as good Catholics, the Portuguese missionaries substituted fish for meat at this time of the year, and batter-frying was a popular presentation.

peanut oil

1 egg, beaten

1 cup (250 mL) cold beer

2 Tbsp (30 mL) dry white wine

½ cup (125 mL) flour

¼ cup (60 mL) rice flour

¼ cup (60 mL) cornstarch

variety of vegetables and seafood, cut into bite-sized pieces

Heat peanut oil in a pan or deep fryer until temperature is 375° F (190° C) (see Tip). Combine egg, beer and wine in a small bowl.

In another bowl, combine flour, rice flour and cornstarch. Add liquid to dry mixture and very lightly mix together. The batter should look lumpy. Dip vegetables and seafood in tempura batter and fry in small batches until golden and crispy.

Tip

For deep-frying, peanut oil should be 2 to 3 in (5 to 7.5 cm) deep in pot or use deep fryer according to the manufacturer's directions.

Tip

The keys to a tasty, crispy tempura are a very light mixing of the batter—lumps are *good*—and using an ice-cold liquid, preferably one that is carbonated. To avoid greasy, soggy tempura, it is important to maintain the proper temperature of the oil, so it's best to have a thermometer on hand.

Traditionally, the Japanese mix their tempura batter with chopsticks, ensuring that it is never overmixed.

Balsamic-glazed Root Vegetables

Serves 4 as a side dish

Because of their excellent keeping qualities, root vegetables are important as winter food. The term "root vegetable" is a general collective term that has come to include all vegetables, from a variety of families, that grow underground; for example, potatoes, carrots, onions, rutabagas and beets. Root vegetables, an important food source for the early settlers of the Prairies, provided vital nourishment for families through the long winters. These vegetables were easy to grow, lasted months on the shelf, and were filling and carbohydrate-dense. Even today, when many exotic imported vegetables are available in winter in our grocery stores, root vegetables remain staples through winter for the same reasons they benefited our ancestors.

Marinade

¼ cup (60 mL) balsamic vinegar

¼ cup (60 mL) extra virgin olive oil or melted butter

2 Tbsp (30 mL) honey

¼ cup (60 mL) fresh parsley, finely chopped

Root Vegetables

1 lb (500 g) baby potatoes, a variety if possible, washed and halved or quartered, depending on size

2 medium parsnips, peeled and quartered lengthwise, then halved

1 medium yam, halved and sliced ¼ in (6 mm) thick

(continued on next page)

Preheat oven to 375° F (190° C). Combine marinade ingredients and set aside.

Place potatoes, parsnips, yam, beet, carrot, garlic and onion into a large mixing bowl. Pour prepared marinade over top, season with salt and pepper and toss to coat. Place into 9 x 13 in (23 x 33 cm) pan and assemble thyme and rosemary sprigs on top. Roast uncovered, turning once or twice, for about 45 minutes or until edges are golden brown and vegetables can be pierced easily with a knife. Toss with fresh parsley and serve.

The reduced balsamic vinegar in this dish enhances the earthy flavour of winter vegetables.

Balsamic vinegar is an aged reduction sauce that originates from Modena, Italy. The best balsamic vinegar is aged a long time, comes in very small bottles and is very expensive. Instead, try a cheaper variety but not the cheapest—it's most likely just red vinegar with brown sugar or caramel.

1 small beet, washed and quartered with skin on

1 large carrot, peeled and quartered lengthwise, then halved

1 bulb garlic, broken into cloves, peeled and left whole

1 small yellow onion, peeled and quartered

sea salt and freshly ground pepper to taste

2 sprigs fresh thyme

2 sprigs fresh rosemary

Brandied Seville Marmalade with Lemon and Ginger

Makes 4 x 1 cup (250 mL) jars

In the Prairies, you will find Seville oranges in your local grocery stores as early as late December through to February, also an ideal time for making jams and marmalades and lifting your spirits during these cold winter months. Closely related to the Bergamot orange, which is used to flavour Earl Grey tea, the Seville orange is a species of bitter orange (*Citrus aurantium*) that originated in Vietnam. Inedible fresh, the Seville orange is prized for making marmalades, compotes and liqueurs, and is the traditional ingredient in duck a l'orange. Because it was the Spaniards who first introduced this orange to the New World, it became associated with the famous Spanish city of Seville, where many of the streets are lined with Seville orange trees.

2 lbs (1 kg) Seville oranges (about 6), halved crosswise

2 lemons, halved crosswise

⅔ cup (150 mL) candied ginger, thinly sliced

water

sugar

⅓ cup (75 mL) brandy (optional)

Place a 12 in (30 cm) square of dampened cheesecloth in a bowl. Squeeze juice from Seville oranges and lemons into cheesecloth-lined bowl; using spoon or grapefruit knife, scoop seeds and pulp into bowl and tightly tie cheesecloth. Strain juice.

With a sharp knife, thinly slice orange and lemon peel. Combine peel, candied ginger and juice in a large measuring cup. Add an equal amount of water and pour into a large, heavy-bottomed pot. Place pulp-seed bag into pot and bring to a boil over high heat. Reduce heat; cook gently, uncovered, stirring occasionally, for about 2 hours until peel is tender and mixture is reduced. If desired, cover and let stand refrigerated at this stage.

Squeeze out liquid from cheesecloth bag before discarding. (If bag is too hot to handle, let it cool a little.) Measure remaining cooked peel and liquid together and place in a clean pot. Stir in an equal amount of sugar. Bring to a rapid boil, stirring often until marmalade thickens (see Wrinkle Test, opposite). Remove from heat and skim

Savory marmalades can also be made with onions or horseradish.

off foam. Add brandy and stir marmalade continuously for 5 minutes to ensure rind is evenly dispersed. Ladle into hot, sterilized jars to within ¼ in (6 mm) of top rim. Wipe jar rim and apply lids and rings until fingertip tight; do not overtighten. Process jars in a boiling water canner for 5 minutes. Let rest at room temperature until set.

Wrinkle Test

Remove marmalade from heat, place a spoonful of marmalade on a plate that has been chilled in the freezer and return it to chill for one minute. To test, push your finger into the marmalade on the chilled plate; it will form a wrinkle when the right consistency has been reached. If marmalade gel is insufficient, return mixture to a rolling boil and test again.

Molasses Muffins

Makes 12 muffins

Molasses is a by-product of sugar production. It was the most common household sweetener up until the late 19th century because refined sugar cost so much. In fact, the high cost of refined sugar was why so many recipes—old-fashioned favourites such as ginger cookies and cakes, shoofly pie, baked beans and taffy—feature molasses and are still common today. There are three types of molasses on the market: unsulphured, sulphured and blackstrap. Unsulphured molasses is the highest quality and most pure molasses. Blackstrap molasses, which should also be unsulphured, is an excellent source of iron and is high in calcium and copper. Sulphured molasses should be avoided. Most molasses is derived from sugar cane, but it can also be made from sugar beets *(Beta vulgaris* subspecies *vulgaris),* which are grown across the Canadian Prairies.

1¼ cups (310 mL) bran cereal

1½ cups (375 mL) buttermilk

¾ cup (175 mL) molasses

½ cup (125 mL) canola oil or sunflower oil

1 egg, beaten

⅔ cup (150 mL) pitted dates, chopped

1¾ cups (425 mL) flour

1 Tbsp (15 mL) baking powder

1 tsp (5 mL) baking soda

pinch of salt

Preheat oven to 400° F (200° C) and spray a muffin tin with nonstick spray. Set aside. In a bowl, mix cereal and buttermilk and let stand for 5 minutes. Add molasses, oil and egg, and stir to combine. Stir in dates. Set aside.

In another bowl, sift together dry ingredients. Fold dry ingredients into wet until just combined, then fill each muffin tin almost full with batter. Bake for 12 to 15 minutes or until tops of muffins spring back with light pressure. Allow to cool for 5 minutes and then remove from pan.

Tip

Buttermilk and sour milk are often used interchangeably in recipes. To make your own sour milk, put 2 to 3 tsp (5 to 10 mL) of lemon juice or vinegar in a measuring cup and add enough milk for 1 cup (250 mL) of liquid. Let the mixture sit for about 10 minutes.

Sunflower Granola

Makes about 11½ cups (2.9 L)

A perfect start to a cold, dark winter morning, granola first became popular in the 1960s with the hippie movement. There is no right or wrong way to make granola, and it is suited to many ingredients. The sunflower seed featured in this granola is the only oilseed native to the northern Great Plains of North America. Sunflower has been grown in Canada for the commercial market since the early 1940s. Sunflower (*Helianthus annuus*) is grown domestically and commercially throughout the Prairies, with research into the plant taking place in Brooks, Alberta, and Winnipeg and Morden in Manitoba. A great summer project for kids is to plant some sunflower seeds and track the growth of the plant.

4 cups (1 L) old-fashioned oats (not quick)

1 cup (250 mL) unsweetened, shredded coconut

1 cup (250 mL) dried fruit of choice: blueberries, cherries, sliced apricots, etc.

1 cup (250 mL) pumpkin seeds

1½ cups (375 mL) sunflower seeds

½ cup (125 mL) sesame seeds

1 cup (250 mL) wheat germ

1 cup (250 mL) chopped almonds

½ cup (125 mL) chopped cashews

⅔ cup (150 mL) maple syrup

1 tsp (5 mL) pure vanilla extract

½ tsp (2 mL) salt

¼ cup (60 mL) sunflower oil

Preheat oven to 325° F (160° C). Place all ingredients in a large bowl and mix well. Spread on a baking sheet and bake for 15 minutes. Stir and bake 10 more minutes. Stir again and bake 5 to 10 minutes more until golden brown. Cool and store in an airtight container for up to a month.

Tip

Sprinkle granola over your favourite cereal or yogurt, or simply enjoy with milk. You can also eat it plain by the handful, or you can freeze it for use at another time.

Bow Island, home of Alberta Sunflower Seeds Ltd. and the Spitz brand, has a 9.1-metre (30-foot) high statue of a sunflower plant.

Spiced Rum Pear Cake

Serves 12

The origin of the pear can be traced back to Asia, specifically western China. Although many types of pears won't tolerate the cold winters of the Prairies, there are a few hardy varieties that do quite well here, including Ure, David, Golden Spice and John. Pears are picked before they are ripe because, unlike most fruit, they become mushy around the core if they're left on the tree to ripen. Pears ripen from the inside out, so you can't necessarily judge the ripeness by the colour; if you can jiggle the stem of a pear, it is ripe. This simple yet delicious spice cake from the Company's Coming collection will make your afternoon cup of coffee special.

¼ cup (60 mL) butter (or hard margarine)

¼ cup (60 mL) + ⅔ cup (150 mL) brown sugar, packed

2 cups (500 mL) diced peeled pear

¼ cup (60 mL) chopped dried cherries

⅓ cup (75 mL) butter (or hard margarine), softened

2 large eggs

½ cup (125 mL) sour cream

2 Tbsp (30 mL) spiced rum (or orange juice)

½ tsp (2 mL) grated orange zest

½ tsp (2 mL) vanilla extract

1¼ cups (310 mL) all-purpose flour

½ tsp (2 mL) baking powder

¼ tsp (1 mL) baking soda

¼ tsp (1 mL) ground cinnamon

¼ tsp (1 mL) salt

Melt butter in medium saucepan on medium. Add ¼ cup (60 mL) brown sugar. Heat and stir until brown sugar is dissolved.

Add pear and cherries. Cook for about 5 minutes, stirring often, until pear is tender.

Beat butter and ⅔ cup (150 mL) brown sugar in large bowl until light and fluffy.

Add eggs, 1 at a time, beating well after each addition. Add sour cream, rum, orange zest and vanilla extract. Beat well.

Combine flour, baking powder, baking soda, cinnamon and salt in medium bowl. Add to butter mixture in 2 additions, mixing well after each addition until no dry flour remains. Add pear mixture. Stir until just combined. Spread in greased 9 in (23 cm) round pan. Bake in a 350° F (175° C) oven for about 45 minutes until wooden pick inserted in centre comes out clean. Let stand in pan on wire rack until cool.

 *Every spice cake recipe involves a different combination of spices. Some that are commonly used include cinnamon, ginger and nutmeg. Experiment with different combinations and find the one that you like the best.*

Angel Food Cake with Passion Fruit Sauce

Serves 6 to 8

Angel food cake is the quintessential "recovery from the holiday-binge" dessert! This fat-free cake is soft, airy and light. It is difficult to pin down its origin, but it likely first appeared in the late 19th century. Some people attribute angel food cake to the Pennsylvania Dutch, mainly because of their history of using special moulds to form festive cakes. Angel food cake is rare among desserts in that it is fat-free—in fact, it must be kept completely away from oils or fats (including stray bits of egg yolk) in order to achieve its characteristic spongy lightness. Before starting, is vital that all your utensils and bowls be squeaky clean.

1 cup (250 mL) sifted cake flour

1½ cups (375 mL) berry sugar, divided into two ¾ cup (175 mL) portions

¼ tsp (1 mL) sea salt

12 egg whites

1½ tsp (7 mL) vanilla or almond extract

¼ cup (60 mL) warm water

1½ tsp (7 mL) cream of tartar

Passion Fruit Sauce

⅓ cup (75 mL) unsweetened apple juice

1 cup (250 mL) sugar

1 cup (250 mL) fresh passion fruit pulp, from about 6 passion fruit

juice of ½ lemon

Preheat oven to 375° F (190° C). Sift flour, half of sugar and salt 3 times. Set aside. In an electric mixer, beat egg whites, vanilla or almond extract, water and cream of tartar at medium-high speed until foamy. Slowly sift in remaining sugar, beating until peaks are medium-firm.

Sift about ½ cup (125 mL) of flour mixture over egg white mixture and gently fold just until flour disappears. Repeat, folding in remaining flour mixture ½ cup (125 mL) at a time. Pour batter into an ungreased 10 in (25 cm) angel food pan. Bake until cake springs back when lightly touched, about 30 to 40 minutes. Invert pan on a cooling rack or on neck of a bottle in order to maintain as much volume or height of the cake as possible. Cool completely.

For passion fruit sauce, bring apple juice and sugar to a boil in a saucepan and cook over medium heat for about 15 minutes or until thick and syrupy. Add passion fruit pulp and lemon juice and boil for another 3 minutes and remove from heat. Pour sauce into a clean jar and refrigerate up to a week.

Serve cooled cake with passion fruit sauce.

Passion flower (Passiflora) *grows here as an annual woody vine, but the fruit of the species is not as tasty as the tropical species that is available in our grocery stores in the late fall and winter.*

Bloody Caesar

Serves 1

Known unofficially as Canada's national drink, this concoction was invented by Walter Chell in Calgary in 1969. As the head bartender at the Calgary Inn, what is now the Westin Hotel, he was asked to come up with a new drink to celebrate the opening of a new Italian restaurant on the premises. Chell experimented for three months to find the right combination and finally settled on hand-mashed clams, tomato juice, vodka, Worcestershire sauce, salt and pepper, with a celery stick for garnish. To spare bartenders and drinkers the hassle of mashing clams every time a Bloody Caesar was ordered, American entrepreneur Duffy Mott soon developed Clamato juice with Chell's assistance, and now Canadians drink about 350 million Caesars every year. Several kinds of Clamato juice are available, with different levels of spiciness to suit your palate.

1 oz (30 mL) vodka

Clamato juice, as needed

dash of Worcestershire sauce

dash of Tabasco

sea salt and pepper to taste

celery salt

1 stalk celery

Rim a tall glass with celery salt. Add vodka and fill glass with Clamato juice. Add remaining ingredients and stir, then garnish with celery stalk.

Pepper Vodka

To make your own pepper vodka to use in this recipe, simply toast 1/3 cup (75 mL) whole peppercorns in a dry pot over medium-low heat until their aroma is released, about 2 minutes. Remove from heat, and pour a bottle of good-quality clear vodka into pot. Let infuse for 1 hour, then pour back into bottle, including pepper. Keep in freezer (where all vodka should be stored).

Calgary Red Eye or Saskatchewan Red Eye

A mixture very popular in the southern Prairies, a Calgary or Saskatchewan Red Eye is 1 part tomato juice and 2 parts beer.

P'tit Caribou

Serves many!

Early traders in Alberta would mix the ingredients for this very alcoholic beverage together in an earthenware jug and bury it to age it. The name, "little caribou," is said to come from the red colour that reminded the hunters of caribou blood. The recipe given here is a traditional version, but one modernized P'tit Caribou calls for red wine, whisky, crème de cassis and—surprise, surprise—maple syrup.

Mix ingredients together and age for at least 48 hours, refrigerated.

40 oz (1.18 L) white alcohol such as vodka

40 oz (1.18 L) sherry, port or red wine

Index

About the Authors

Canadian chef **Jennifer Ogle** learned her craft from a variety of sources, among them the renowned French cooking school La Varenne, which lead to an opportunity to work in the Michelin-starred restaurant La Madeleine in Burgundy, France. Jennifer recalls that her love of cooking started at an early age, when many Sunday afternoons were spent experimenting in the kitchen. Today, Jennifer enjoys all aspects of the culinary world, from cooking to writing, with a particular passion for seasonal, local ingredients.

James Darcy is a self-confessed epicure whose food and travel interests have taken him around the world. A dedicated researcher into food and culinary techniques, he is also passionate about food folklore.

Jean Paré started her official culinary career as a caterer in Vermilion, Alberta, before going on to found Company's Coming and become Canada's most popular cookbook author—selling 30 million books! Her story appears on p. 4.